CADZOW-HACZOW BOOKS

TOWARDS A MINDFUL SOCIETY

Martin Stepek was born in Scotland, at Cambuslang near Glasgow on 19 February 1959. He started writing while at school but never sought to publish. Instead he began his career as a company director in his father's family business. It was not until 2012 at the age of 53 that he published his first book, the epic poem *For There is Hope*, followed by *Mindful Living* (2014), *Mindful Poems* (2015) and *Mindful Living 2* (2015). He collaborated online with the Polish-American poet John Guzlowski, resulting in their joint volume of micro poems *Waiting for Guzlowski* (2017). His latest works are *A Pocket Guide to a Mindful Life* (2018), *Steps to a Mindful Life* (2018) and *Towards a Mindful Society* (2018).

By the same author

For There is Hope
Mindful Living
Mindful Poems
Mindful Living 2
Waiting for Guzlowski
A Pocket Guide to a Mindful Life
Steps to a Mindful Life
Towards a Mindful Society: The Sunday Herald Collection

MARTIN STEPEK

Towards a Mindful Society:
The Sunday Herald Collection

CADZOW-HACZOW BOOKS

CADZOW-HACZOW BOOKS

Published in Cadzow-Haczow Books 2018

Printed in Great Britain
Copyright © Martin Stepek 2018

Contents

Introduction

In mid-January 2017 I started writing my first column for the Sunday Herald. Aside from Christmas Day and Hogmanay the most important date on a traditional Scot's calendar is Robert Burns' Night, so I thought it both timely and appropriate to start my new column with a mindful reflection on one of the Bard's most evocative and poignant poems, To a Mouse. It appeared in the Sunday Herald's Life magazine on 29th January 2017 alongside a picture of the great poet himself.

So began what was to become the first regular column on mindfulness in a Scottish or British newspaper, and possibly the only one ever to have existed globally. It was a genuine privilege to write it and I was granted near total freedom to take it in any direction I wanted. So I moved reflections on mindfulness into the territories of history, family heritage, music, poetry and national identity as well as the more expected themes of mental health and our myriad states of mind.

All good things though come to an end. So when the Sunday Herald ceased publication on Sunday 2nd September 2018 so too did my first venture into professional journalism with a national newspaper.

When I shared the news on social media I received some beautiful comments about how much people enjoyed the column and benefited from it.

So it was from this groundswell of opinion that I felt the articles should be collected into one volume so that those who enjoyed it first time around could have them all in one place whilst those who missed them first time around could try them albeit in a different format.

Of course I hope you enjoy the contents of this book whether they are new to you or not. Just remember while you read this book however that mindfulness is a way or living, a way of manage and enjoy life in the preciousness of each moment, so do at least occasionally put the book aside and practice what I hope I teach here.

Martin Stepek
November 2018

A Mindful View of *To a Mouse*

Wee, sleekit, cowran, tim'rous beastie,
O, what a panic's in thy breastie!

In the lead up to Burns' Night we'll hear the standard views of Robert Burns as a great humanist, a womaniser, and most of all, a great poet. But there's a couple of aspects of Burns' nature that I don't think have been explored in depth, aspects that relate to a wider compassion and an instinct understanding of the benefits of being mindful.

Being mindful is noticing what's actually going on in the present moment so that we can enjoy our moments more in real time. This can be external things: what we see, hear, touch, smell and taste, but also the inner stuff: our thoughts, impulses, gut reactions, moods, and emotions. A body of high level scientific study is increasingly showing that if we sharpen our mindfulness in everyday life we become clearer in our thinking, feel much calmer, are more resilient under pressure, and show more compassion towards others. It rekindles a joy of life, something many of us have lost in the throes of our everyday modern frantic world.

Poetry is often described as heightened awareness. Mindfulness develops this directly.

Wee, sleekit, cowran, tim'rous beastie.

Burns is recollecting the fear in a mouse. The poet had accidentally overturned the little shelter it had built to protect itself from winter's chills.

This is a scene of utmost compassion. Let's run through it in slow motion, mindfully, as if time has slowed down so you can notice more.

Burns sees the mouse.

He notices its scurrying and understands immediately what he has done.

Immediately in his heart he feels compassion for it.

These are three linked but distinct mental activities: seeing, understanding, feeling.

Notice that the compassion is automatic. Farmers are much closer to nature than we are. For some that constant awareness of the realities of nature can bring a coldness to the heart. Life comes and goes. But for others, like Burns, the poignancy and fragility of life enhances his innate compassion.

Your own mind works in the same way. You notice things with your senses. The brain processes what you experience in order to assess it. Then it may or may not produce an automatic response.

From a mindfulness perspective the automatic response is the problem. We are all programmed by a combination of genes, upbringing, culture, and the times we live in. We don't get to choose these. This makes us much more of an automaton that we think we are.

We think we're intelligent, reasoning people, making decisions based on thoughtful assessments of situation. But scientific evidence shows otherwise. Most of our responses happen without our conscious input. As Einstein once put it, by the time we're eighteen we're a bundle of prejudices.

Some of these prejudices are good. Burns was programmed to be kind and thoughtful to creatures in trouble.

Mindfulness enables us to deprogramme what is unhealthy, and if we want, to programme new responses to life. Burns had close to a universal compassion. It's a view that everything that lives and can feel pain and pleasure should be left unharmed where possible, and helped, nurtured and revered as part of this remarkable thing we call life.

I'm truly sorry Man's dominion
Has broken Nature's social union,
An' justifies that ill opinion,
Which makes thee startle,
At me, thy poor, earth-born companion,
An' fellow-mortal!

Burns recognises the mouse's equal right to life and security. The words "thy poor earth-born companion, an' fellow mortal" are, to my mind, an exquisite pronouncement of universal love. And what Burns had inside him by chance we can consciously develop.

Simply being more mindful seems to enhance compassion because as we see and hear more clearly we notice others' suffering, which often ignites fellow-feeling. But we can choose to go further. There's a practice the Buddha developed which has been adapted to a secular form and it enhances our compassion.

When you have a quiet moment think of someone or something still alive that you love or like. See if you can gently stay with your feeling, allowing it to soak into you more deeply. Notice what this feels like and enjoy it. Then express a wish that the person or animal be happy and safe. See if you can feel your love and kindness towards them. Stay with it for a while then accept when the feeling fades. The practice is finished.

You can go further and see if you can bring a sense of compassion towards someone you know who is suffering right now in their life. Bring them to your mind. Bring awareness of their suffering condition, perhaps physical pain, exhaustion, fear or uncertainty. Try not to sink into suffering alongside the person, but rather nurture the wish to help the person. Then just sit with that wish to be kind and let it soak into you. Notice and enjoy it.

In this way, slowly but surely you can develop greater compassion, maybe in time to a poetic level. If you set aside a few minutes each day to do this practice you'll be surprised at how quickly your sense of compassion and awareness grows.

Finally, remember to enjoy life in the moment. Burns expressed in the last lines of this beautiful poem the nub of the problem; our tendency to be distracted from the present to past pains and future fears.

Still, thou art blest, compar'd wi' me!
The present only toucheth thee:
But Och! I backward cast my e'e,
On prospects drear!
An' forward, tho' I canna see,
I guess an' fear!

I'm certain we'll return to these subjects again.

Baggage Galore

There's an old story – from China I think - about two Zen priests out for a walk. They come to the banks of a shallow river where there's an elderly woman who wants to cross the river but fears she might slip on a rock, hit her head, and drown. I know; it's already sexist and ageist but that's the way with old stories so bear with me.

Zen priests at that time were strictly forbidden to touch a woman. One of the priests explained this to the woman but despite this rule, the other priest offered to carry her across. The woman accepted, so the priest safely took her across safely.

When the two priests resumed their walk the priest who refused to touch the woman reprimanded his friend for breaking a vow of the Order. Half an hour later he was still telling him off, explaining why the rules exist and why, no matter the situation, you should stick to them.

The priest who had carried the woman across suddenly laughed out loud.

"What's so funny?" asked his friend, annoyed that the other was not appreciating the seriousness of the offence.

"Well I let go of that old woman ages ago but you still seem to be carrying her around with you. And it's weighing you down."

With life comes stuff. Good stuff, like doing well in an exam, getting a job we wanted, falling in love, becoming a parent, the last payment of a mortgage after twenty-five years of paying, seeing your kids grow up. And bad stuff. Little bad stuff like losing a friend over some petty argument, or getting the Christmas present we wanted, or not getting the promotion we had applied for. And really, really bad stuff. A contentious divorce, the death of a child, a family suicide, sexual abuse, physically violent abuse, serious illness, and stuff not many of us thankfully have witnessed – war, torture, the destruction of our home town.

We have memories. Memories are, according to scientific researchers, very skewed personal takes on something that happened. And we keep them with us, like an internal series of stories and images. Some of the good stuff, some not so good, some bad. In most cases we can live happily, enjoyably and actively with this plethora of memories archived somewhere in the amazing archive system of the brain.

There's the old phrase "forgive and forget". Actually in practical terms it's just as helpful if we can't forgive something but for the most part we do forget about it. In other words it's not getting in our way in our daily life.

In some cases however the baggage we carry with us is unhelpfully heavy, and in extremis weighs us down so much we can barely function.

I remember when it was announced that the English entertainer Roy Castle had terminal cancer and given six months to live. He decided to do a tour, reckoning that if he only had such a limited time left to him he would enjoy it as much as his condition would allow.

Most people given similar bad news go into depression, often severe. They lose much of their will to live even before they lose life itself. That normal and understandable, but it's such a waste of the precious life that was still available to them.

They carried their life sentence around with them, dragged down so heavily that they could barely move. Roy Castle meanwhile, with the exact same pain and challenges played his trumpet, told stories and danced. Danced to the end of love, as the late Leonard Cohen put it.

Mindfulness is noticing what's going on. Inside as well as out. So much of the baggage that we carry about with us ignites, often at random moments, and takes us over for a while. It does so very powerfully, so that we suffer the effect of it without really being aware of how it arose in us.

With the practice of mindfulness we start to get a hang of noticing, quietly, deliberately. Anything will do. Notice the head of the tea through the cup onto your fingers and palms. Or the lovely lubrication that water provides to your throat as you swallow.

Noticing deliberately, without too much intellectual inner commentary or judgements, hones this as a deep-seated, subtle skill. It grows in you almost without you noticing – isn't that ironic? As it develops you start to notice things about yourself that you previously didn't see. Like all the baggage. The pain, the regrets, the suffering, the hatreds, the guilt, the prejudices. A lot of stuff. Ugly stuff. But hey, welcome to the human race. There's a lot of good in you too; kindness, love, forgiveness, humour, insight, creativity. So don't get hung up on the negatives, but do address them.

It comes slowly, the letting go. If you're impatient and annoyed that some baggage doesn't disappear more quickly that is in itself developing more baggage – impatience, frustration, annoyance. They're all forms of baggage too. So if you really want to slowly let this stuff go, be patient, accept its existence in you, while you practice your everyday mindfulness. The time will come when you actually notice the baggage as it arises, and you are able to sit with it in your head, but without it taking you over and poisoning your state of mind. Then you're on the road to decluttering your most toxic forms of baggage. Over time you'll walk more lightly on this world, maybe so lightly you can readily carry some old woman – or man – who needs your help.

Autopilot

According to the futurists we're coming into an age of driverless cars, buses, taxis. So the question often quoted in meetings about who will lead a project, "Who's driving the bus?" may become obsolete but it remains a good metaphor for how our mind influences our lives.

Think of how you drive a car. It's completely habitual, requiring little or no conscious deliberation. We brake, accelerate, check mirrors without even being aware we're doing it. Yet we drive safely.

Compare this with how we drove during our first driving lessons. We were ultra-cautious and absolutely focussed on what was going on moment by moment. This was of course because we were terrified of scratching another car parked at the near side of the road, or colliding with another car coming in the opposite direction.

But another reason we were so focussed was because driving is a complex skill. Two hands are needed to control the steering wheel, yet the left hand has to change gear and pull the handbrake on, while one of the hands occasionally has to switch indicators and wipers on and off.

And that's just the hands. We also have footwork. Two feet but three pedals. How inconvenient.

o we have to regularly switch the right foot from the accelerator to the brake while the left foot does the more occasional task of working the clutch. All while our two hands are doing entirely different tasks.

When you're not used to doing these things it's incredibly difficult. But once your mind gets the hang of it you can drive on motorways for hours barely aware that you're driving when they're driving.

So back to the question "Who's driving the bus?" Who is actually functioning, making decisions, and creating emotions, feelings and moods in your everyday life? It's your mind and it's doing it for the most part automatically, without your conscious input, often in complete contrast to how you would like to think, feel, or behave.

Put simply our brains have evolved to learn skills and responses, and once sufficiently able, it switches off the mindful part of the mind and goes on autopilot. The example of driving a car shows how useful and effective that can be. The problem is that the mind doesn't just learn good habits that way.

Just as we become car drivers on autopilot, so too can anger become an automatic reaction to specific triggers. Or bigotry, prejudice, hate, resentment. Similarly the major mental health epidemics of our times, depression, anxiety and stress all developed from the same mind that learns from experiences and turns certain responses into automatic reactions.

There is a good side to this of course. Our senses of compassion, kindness, altruism, resilience, love, and empathy can also become so frequent a part of our response system that they arise automatically.

The important thing in all this is to realise that we're not actually in control. There is a huge difference between what we think of when we think of "me" and this mind that keeps automatically doing things on our behalf.

From our every single experience, in conjunction with the unique combination of genes we inherited, we become programmed to automatically respond or react in a given way in a particular circumstance. It's quite shocking to realise this. It's not quite no will power but it's pretty close.

However it's not irreversible. In neuroscience the term neuroplasticity has become a big thing, and mindfulness is seen in that field as a major tool for neuroplasticity. Neuroplasticity means that our minds can in fact be reshaped, deprogrammed, freed up.

When we start to try to be mindful we begin to see our automatic responses to everyday things. What someone is wearing. The tone of voice a person uses. Their accent. A political leader on TV. The weather. The thought of a glass of wine when we are tired after coming home from work.

Training in mindfulness – observing what is actually happening in the present moment – gives us the chance to notice our own automatic reactions as they arise.

Once noticed we can consider whether what is in our mind is going to do good or harm. This in turn gives us the possibility of considering alternative thoughts or feelings to the automatic one.

I've done mindfulness sessions in prisons. It's salutary. A prisoner is in jail because of something they did in a single moment. Leave aside the circumstances that led up to the crime, or what they might have done afterwards. Just consider the moment itself. Imagine an altercation. In a moment of anger a knife is pulled and plunged into someone. In a single moment.

In that moment it was possible, with training, to see the rage and the hatred, and instead of pulling the knife, to observe the emotions, the situation, and let things settle down sufficiently for a non-violent finale.
In a mindful moment this needn't have been what transpired. In that mindful moment of not pulling a knife, two families' lives would have gone down different less tragic paths.

I have emails from people saying how a single moment of mindfulness changed a suicide into a life, a divorce into a continued relationship, stress into peace.

In every moment you have an option. To go unthinkingly with whatever pops up in your mind. Or to notice, pause, see what's arisen in your mind.
Gently and kindly see if what's there is good, nurturing, constructive, or if it could lead to outcomes you don't want. In the pause see if something more constructive can come into your mind, and if so choose it.

The world changes in that moment. Subtly, maybe in tiny ways. Instead of continuing to watch the TV when a friend comes in with a baby, you smile at the child, hold it, and say "hello beautiful". This changes the baby. And it changes you.

Every single moment an opportunity. Try not to miss being alive to them.

Mindfulness and Kindness

As we all know life brings its ups and downs. These can be personal issues, family matters, work-related, or to do with the wider world of politics, the economy, the weather and environment.

The sub-branch of neuroscience known as neuro-plasticity has started to help us understand how these life events impact on who we are and how we respond to life moment by moment, day to day.

Neuro means the nerves, which are the pathways by which messages are delivered to and from the brain. Plasticity means the ability to be reshaped. That's where the word plastic gets its origin. When you heat up plastic it melts and in that warms state can be remoulded into any shape. Neuroscience now informs us that our mind, our traits and our personalities can be, to a greater or lesser extent, re-formed.

So what changes us in this way? What reshapes who we are and how we think and act?

The answer, in general terms, is simple: everything our brain perceives through the five senses reshapes us, and everything our brain creates in terms of thoughts, feelings, moods, ideas also adds to the reshaping process.

We are therefore being reshaped moment by moment. Much of the reshaping of the mind is simply reaffirming or strengthening what we know.

So first time we see grass we get the shock of seeing that it is green. However the fifty thousandth time we see grass, the sight of it merely reinforces our expectation that grass will be green. Note though that the reinforcement of that expectation is still a change to the mind.

So this act of constant neuroplasticity or changing of the mind happens whether we like it or not. Think on that for a second. We are being changed by experiences which we very often have no control over, and we have no control either over the type of changes that are made to us.

Mindfulness is a tool of neuroplasticity. It's a skill we can deliberately develop and strengthen to give us a measure of greater control over how we are changed, and in the longer-term to what external and internal factors we allow to be present in our lives and therefore affect us.

When we are mindful in a particular moment we can better perceive the potential or actual consequence of that moment's experience. Let's take an example. You read a highly inflammatory message on Facebook. You recognise your anger, your desire to respond with an insulting retort about the person who wrote the message or their views.

The mindfulness is the self-awareness of your emotional reaction, then awareness of your wish to respond by an aggressive retort.

Now on reflection you might still feel it is the right thing to do to answer as your gut response suggested. At least you have had the chance to consider it. Or you may choose not to respond at all, or to do so in a different manner.

This choice is the gift of being mindful. You move from being automatic, your response dictated to you by your own brain, to choosing amongst options. In that instant you are more free than in the moment before. You are temporarily liberated from your autopilot mind.

But we don't have to wait for events to happen before we try to become mindful and make things better through wiser choices. We know now that certain activities nurture constructive or positive results in life. I'll no doubt focus on some of these in more detail another time but they include obvious things like exercise, being in nature, eating types of food. So we can deliberately choose to do things that improve our lives, in particular moments. We develop our mindfulness to the extent that it is looking out for opportunities to improve our wellbeing, even in single moments.

One of the most effective and, to my mind, most beautiful of all human actions, is kindness. We can make a point of trying to develop our mindfulness to notice if we can be kind in any given situation rather than just looking out for our own self-interest.

Forgetting for a moment the positive impact that acts of kindness have on the receiver, let's look at what science tells us about how acts of kindness impact on the giver. Here is just a selection, all demonstrated repeatedly by research:

The giver feels happier
Decrease of stress hormones
Increased sense of vitality
Strengthened immune system
Lowers blood pressure
A longer life
A greater sense of meaning and purpose in life

In other words if kindness was a pill it'd be given out as a prescription to virtually all of us. It results in both mental and physical health benefits, and of course benefits the person you are helping. That person not only gets the benefit of your direct help, but also a renewed sense that other people can be good, thus restoring one's faith in human nature.

The opposite is generally true too. Being unkind harms our mental and physical health, and removes the possibility of another person feeling better about life and people; so unkindness is both a form of self-harm and the loss of an opportunity to make mankind a little bit more positive about each other.

We can deliberately cultivate awareness of opportunities to be kind. Even simple things like putting a post-it note saying – Remember, be kind - on a corner of our computer or by the phone can trigger the mindfulness to consider this type of response as an alternative to the automatic mind's reaction to emails or other messages.

Using these two marvellous tools in conjunction – mindfulness to hone the awareness, then kindness as a two-way nurturing response – can build up to become something deeply beneficial in your life.

Love and Loss

My Aunt Zosia died last week in London. She was 92. In one sense I hardly knew her, having only visited her once as an adult, and barely remembered her from my childhood. In another way though I knew her inside out, knew her suffering, her kindness and how much she lost in her life. I have written about these things, spoken about them, put her image on Powerpoint slides. I made her the main subject of my mindfulness talk last week at the free class I do every Tuesday evening at the UWS campus in my home town of Hamilton. A decade ago I went down to London and filmed her for hours, asking her absolutely everything I could about her extraordinary life, especially her years spent in the Soviet labour camp system and subsequent five thousand mile odyssey to freedom, in Persia.

She told me how she cradled a little girl in a mud hut in Uzbekistan that was being used as a makeshift hospital, and how the little girl, her panic subsided by Zosia's soothing, died in her arms. Zosia was seventeen at the time.

She told me how she risked her life to save her little sister, bartering a small loaf of bread in an Uzbeki village for grapes, having snuck out of the camp she was in and walked alone in the wintry cold to the nearest village to enact her deal. A nurse had told her that only grapes or similar fruit could possibly save her sister's life but that there was no fruit in the desolate camp.

Back in her tent she cut each grape in half and holding her sister's head in her other arm, squeezed the juice through the parched, barely open lips, all night long. Her sister recovered and is still alive.

How do we cope with loss? Unless we go first, we'll all have to face it time after time. Better to prepare for it than face the shock. That's what the Tibetan Buddhists taught me a long time ago now.

Really understand death. The practice they taught me which I still use in an adapted form, was to make it a part of a twenty-one day cycle of different themes on which to reflect, and deepen in our mind. So once every three weeks for close to twenty years I have taken time out to get to know death better. My own, my closest family members, the people I love most, but also strangers, animals, birds, fish, you name it, all that lives and therefore is going to die.

Cheery stuff.

Well actually it turns out to be exactly that.

But before I go any further let me deal with this word "meditation". I avoid using it except to say why I don't like it. Its origin, in the context of this article, was in the ancient Indian language, Pali. Their word for it was *bhavana* (rhymes with banana). It meant the development of our mental state. It's very clear.

The word *meditation* on the other hand may describe a thousand different practices, from unproven New Age mantras to scientifically-researched secular mental training. In the absence of a pithy word like *bhavana* in English I just say my practices are for mental development.

Back to death. Give yourself some quiet mental space to allow your mind to gently but deeply examine death, what it is, how you feel about it, what you fear about it, how unpredictable it is in terms of when and how it comes. When you just allow these things to arise in your mind, regularly, without panic, without running away from it, without denial, you slowly become at peace with it.

I don't fear death. I don't mind if I'm gone before this is published. C'est la vie, or rather c'est la mort.

Don't get me wrong. I'd love to live healthily, with whatever intelligence I have now, up to and past the age of a hundred. There's a lot I think I can do to help others if I am given more time, but it has taken me decades to realise how best to do it, so if I am lucky enough to have more time I can now do some good things effectively.

In addition I'd love to spend decades more with my family, help my children, see them develop.

I'd love to write more books, explore how we can overcome some of our current horrors like foodbanks and homelessness in Scotland, and starvation and war globally.

But if it doesn't happen, it doesn't happen.

Also, not fearing death doesn't mean I don't fear pain or the often horrible process of dying. But I'm not in a position to choose that given that I want to live for as long and as well as I can.

But to cheery things. Reflecting on death, allowing the mind to softly and non-judgementally absorb more deeply into the subject can, eventually, lead to an incredibly deep and rich appreciation of life; of just being alive; and a stronger recognition of just how much we love certain people, places, things.

From this growing appreciation comes joy. Joy of being alive. It's an amazing feeling. From joy you gain poetic insights that marvel at being alive, at ordinary things. As William Blake put it so beautifully:

To see a World in a Grain of Sand
And a Heaven in a Wild Flower,
Hold Infinity in the palm of your hand
And Eternity in an hour.

Who would not want to see life like that, in everyday moments?

So goodbye my beautiful Aunt Zosia. It was a joy to know you and a privilege to have had you as part of my life. No regrets, no grief.

Just love.

You and Your Mind

"I think therefore I am." Descartes' view has held sway for a long time. It's one of those revered quotes, so familiar it's more like an advertising slogan for the human race than something we should take seriously nowadays. For me it's also a classic statement of human arrogance and superiority. It stems from the idea that only humans have the gift of deliberate thought, that other animals are just dumb instinctive, lesser beings.

It is also extremely harsh on those people who through an accident or a genetic disorder seem incapable of thought. Think on it. If you are only you because you are capable of thought, because you can reason and explore ideas, create new concepts, then what about those who can't?

Yet this view of us as a species that is defined as being capable of thinking independently, freely, without limitations is plain wrong, at least in part.

A Harvard study a few years ago found that our mind is distracted on average about 47% of the time. By distraction they meant that the mind was not where we expected or wanted it to be. So as an example imagine you're reading this article when you start to think about the fact that your car is getting a bit old and unreliable and maybe you need a new one.

You wanted to stay focussed on reading this but your mind just took you away from it, without your consent, possibly even without your conscious awareness that you had started thinking about your car.

We could therefore rephrase Descartes. "I think therefore I get distracted half my life." Or "I think sometimes but half the time my mind does what it wants to do whether I like it or not". Granted neither of these are as pithy or profound sounding as Descartes' version but at least now we're on real solid ground.

We are far more conditioned than we think we are. Ironically we don't think we are conditioned precisely because we are conditioned not to think we are conditioned. This is the absence of mindfulness. We are being dragged continually by thoughts, moods and emotions rather than us being in control of what the mind thinks, feels and chooses in any circumstance.

Think about it right now. Who gets angry when you get angry? Who chooses to feel depressed? Or anxious? Or hateful? Who decides that they'll carry a grudge around with them for thirty years or more?

Who chooses to be a bigot, a racist, sexist, ageist?

It's not you, or at least not the reasoning, intelligent, thoughtful you that Descartes suggests, because no reasoning intelligent, thoughtful person would every allow these toxic moods or views anywhere near their precious mind.

Imagine Descartes was right. Imagine we really could be capable of total control over our thoughts, which include our feelings, moods, emotions, gut reactions. What would most of us choose to feel like? I'd imagine we'd love to feel fulfilled, happy, have a sense of joy of life, a sense of purpose and meaning. Most of us would also like everyone else to feel that way, including our leaders in government and business, so that a decent, secure, happy and purposeful society would develop.

The Buddha got it so much more accurately than Descartes. "With our thoughts we create the world." That's extraordinarily profound. It's also scary, because if we're not in control of our thoughts and where they take us, the world we create with those thoughts can become horrific. What we are witnessing in our world right now, with the resurrection of openly racist and in some cases literally neo-fascist views, can only have arisen as the result of people's thoughts.

So if you want just a happy life for yourself, free from worries, anxiety, depression, anger, resentment, bitterness and a score of other harmful and often self-destructive moods and emotions, you need to train your mind so it becomes less automatic, less conditioned, less distracted, and in its place, more under your direct control.

And if a good society or a sane, fruitful world is to become a reality this will require billions of people developing control over their minds so that they do not fall prey to the influence of hateful demagogues. It starts with you. I know dozens of people who are politically engaged and active ion what we'd call progressive campaigns, know what they oppose, and know what their idea of a good society is. But they're not in charge even of their own minds, let alone able to convince others to change theirs. They display hatred and a total absence of compassion for their political opponents, celebrate every minor mistake the "enemy" makes, and generally demonstrate precisely the attitudes that they believe we need to eradicate if society is to improve.

If you want a love of life, which is simply a state of mind, you have to develop it. If you want peace of mind then do the work that brings you closer to it. Do not accept being a semi-automaton.

If you want a good society then it really does start with you. Gandhi was another one who got it right. "Be the change you want to see in this world". You could add, more obviously "Train yourself so that you become the change you want to see in yourself". Or in the words of another social radical "first cast out the beam out of thine own eye; and then shalt thou see clearly to cast out the mote out of thy brother's eye".

Make Space for Mental Space

We live in unexplored territory. The human mind has never had so much to notice or absorb in the sixteen or seventeen hours of wakefulness we have each day. I'm fifty-eight, so I remember when there were two television channels, and neither of them was on all day long. No internet, no emails, phone calls were so expensive you had to ask your parents' permission to use the one phone in the house. So boredom was far more likely for children and adults alike than overload.

I'm not one of the plethora of people who bemoan social media or the increasing use of technology. I've seen the best side of it when my family and our cousins in Australia kept each other in touch with developments as our respective mothers – who were sisters – slowly got increasingly ill and died. Mutual love and support, sympathy and grief flowed through the family Facebook group we created specifically for that purpose. It was an amazing experience, one we've kept up and added to, bringing in wider family, many of whom we had never previously been in contact with, some of whom have still never met face to face.

What concerns me is use of time. Time is all we have, and it's a bit ungraspable. I instinctively think of time like a succession beads on a string. In other words something tangible followed by another identical thing then another and so on.

But time isn't like that at all. It just is. It's an experience of the mind. By the time you even stop to think about what a moment is, it's gone, seemingly to be replaced by another moment, then another. You can't pin it down. But if you contemplate it looking backwards in time, you see something utterly different. Those moments are always lost to us. Used, misused, or unused, they're gone, and can't be retrieved. How many of us occasionally find ourselves thinking of a past event and wishing we could go back in time and change it?

In reality each of us is unique. Equally however, the vast majority of us do similar sorts of things and have similar priorities in everyday life. Most people have to work to earn a living, we spend a lot of time watching TV, usually news, dramas, soap operas, and comedies according to the viewing figures. We spend hours on the internet, with social media now a significant part of our day. Apart from sleeping, eating, and washing ourselves these few groups of activities – work, television viewing, internet engagement – take up the bulk of our week days.

This jars with surveys of what matters most to us. What matters most is not work (except for the necessity of having to earn a living), television, the news, or social media. It's our physical health, our sense of wellbeing and purpose, and the health and happiness of our immediate family and closest friends. Those are the things people say matter most to them.

In a nutshell we want to attain one lot of things but in our actual lives do a series of things that don't seem too related to these deepest aspirations.

To my mind the problem is not the internet, not social media, not the television. It's the mind that has incrementally over decades been programmed by life, by society, by osmosis, to seek out these things rather than the things our deepest and most rational mind knows we need and want. Eventually they become unthinking daily habits.

The practice of mindfulness says, first just notice. This purpose of this column is to remind you to do this, then to act on what you notice.

When you notice that your mind is fixed on something irrelevant or even potentially harmful, then see if you can just stop for a few moments. Stop and notice more clearly what you're doing and allow your mind to remember what you really want to do. Compare the two. If that means you then put down this magazine or switch off the computer you're reading this on, get changed into a tracksuit and go for a run, that's exactly what mindfulness urges us to do.

You can go back to the column later, but your health is more important... except that this column is specifically designed to help you with an even more important thing in your life - your mental health, your sense of joy of life. So maybe finish reading this first, soak in the importance of what it contains, then go and improve your fitness.

A day ends; and although it may seem like a pain in the neck to eat five or ten veg and fruit a day, do your high intensity cardio work or more traditional run, swim or cycle, if you don't do it today then you've lost today's chance to be as well as you can.

Simply stop for moments dotted through the day, and notice the grass, the sounds of birds, the fact that you have clean water from a tap, or any of a thousand things you can notice in a typical day. Maybe even forfeit one television programme to give you that space in each day. You will blossom as a human being. A day will gradually become a thing of inherent value and of utter beauty, and that will contribute immensely to your wellbeing. That television programme you gave up? The day will come when you can't even remember what it was called.

Wabi-Sabi

So Jessica Alba follows the philosophy or way of life called Wabi-Sabi. So does Will-i-am; and the tabloids are either loving it as the latest fad for celebs, or mocking it as yet another New Age junk for the gullible middle-classes who have nothing better to do with their lives.

The sensible approach is of course to investigate it, if you want, and see what it actually is in reality, as opposed to our knee-jerk reactions as soon as we hear about it.

So where does Wabi-Sabi come from and what is it all about?

The Buddha taught that everything comes and goes, that nothing is permanent, indeed that, as Heraclitus put it "no man steps in the same river twice". This notion, that everything changes, crumbles and dies is at the heart of Wabi-Sabi.

Through a period of hundreds of years Buddhism crossed eastwards through Asia and eventually arrived as Zen in Japan via China - the word Zen comes from the Chinese term Chan, and simply means meditation. In China Buddhism was affected by the native philosophy of Taoism to create a more aesthetic form coupled with the strict formality and ritual derived from Confucius's Analects.

In Japan not only did they nurture this remarkably sparse and disciplined form of Buddhism they called Zen, they reformed much of Japanese artistic, architectural and horticultural sensibilities in its wake.

Part of this revolutionary thinking in aesthetics was the idea that things that were imperfect had a beauty or intrigue about them that perfectly formed things don't. This is easy to understand if you consider the appeal of a castle ruins compared to a perfect one. So, for Scots, Urquhart Castle on Loch Ness compared to Culzean Castle.

A typical Japanese example would be allowing moss to grow on rocks in a Japanese garden rather than cleaning the moss off. In our culture we sometimes call this "character".

One of my favourite writers William Somerset Maugham said that when he was young he loved the writings of Jonathan Swift best of all author, but as he grew older he grew irritated by the sheer perfection of Swift's prose.

In sport those of us old enough to remember will see this aesthetic difference of taste reflected in those who preferred rough-cut Steve Ovett compared to smooth, polite Seb Coe.

So that's what Wabi-Sabi is, a recognition and appreciation of imperfection, of the roughness we associate with nature compared to the artificial perfection mankind aims to create in arts, crafts and mass-produced products.

I love it simply because it appeals to my own gut view of things – rough and ready beats polished; but that's a matter of personal taste. For some people finely tuned, perfectly detailed work is what attracts them most.

I find it a bit strange that this way of seeing things and creating them has morphed into a philosophy of sorts. Strange because it is part of an already ancient and very profound philosophy of Zen Buddhism, something practiced daily by millions of people not only in Japan and China but Korea and Vietnam.

However rather than be dismissive of it on the one hand or just rush out and try it out on the other, mindfulness would suggest that we simply look at it, see it for what it is, check out if there's any objective scientific evidence to suggest it is worth practicing.

Aspects associated with Wabi-Sabi are already common-place and accepted. The mindset of perfectionism has been shown for decades to be unhealthy for people, both mentally and physically, so the view within the new version of Wabi-Sabi that we should not strive to make everything perfect is common sense. However it should be recognised that for some people perfectionism is something they deliberately choose despite its negative effects on their health. Consider poor Joseph Heller. He worked on his classic novel Catch 22 for eight years, and it took him thirteen years to finish writing his second novel, ironically titled Something Happened.

Other features of Wabi-Sabi are simple living and slowing down. Neither is new, both are healthy.

For me the best thing about Wabi-Sabi coming into play in its adapted form is that it gives fresh life to the aesthetic and artistic idea of imperfection. It plays to the Dada, minimalist, abstract and absurdist schools of art, and to the eccentric or outsider person in an overwhelmingly conformist and uniform society. In its implied appreciation of everyday things, like grass or puddles, it aligns with a poetic sensibility, as expressed beautifully by Dylan Thomas "The force that through the grew fuse drives the flower / Drives my green age…"

So for me personally it's a welcome new feature for those who look for practical ways to live their lives better. I'm biased of course. For me mindfulness has an edge because it has deep robust evidence for the benefits it can bring us, and it sits within an ethical, psychological and philosophical framework that makes it very coherent and powerful in all aspects of our daily life. And of course Wabi-Sabi, coming from Zen, shares its origins in that self-same intellectual and practical structure. But anything that can bring people greater contentment alongside deeper appreciation of the beauty of everyday life and objects is a good thing, and not something to be disparaged simply because film stars and musicians declare that they live by it.

What do you Need?

My dad was once asked to choose between two things on a table. He chose one. That's why I'm here typing this article. If he had chosen the other I would never have been born, and you would not have had the pleasure of reading this article.

He chose the small dark loaf of bread.

The alternative was to choose a gun. The gun, unlike the bread, would not have been given to him. It was to be used on him, and this was explained to him before he made the choice.

Well, who wouldn't have chosen the bread, especially if you were in such a state of malnutrition that you could almost put your hand round your thigh and touch finger to thumb?

But he lost honour in the process, a humiliating defeat against the enemy. For the man offering the choice on the other side of the table was a KGB officer (then called the NKVD). In order to get the bread my father had to agree to do anything the Soviet Union asked of him for the rest of his life. This was Dad's Room 101 moment, the Orwellian process made to break a person.

Dad reasoned afterwards that what was agreed under duress had no real status, but he knew that at any time in his life there could be a phone call or a knock on the door. Fortunately he died age 90 without ever having to face such a situation.

Mindfulness asks us to be aware of what is going on moment by moment. In my father's scenario it was literally a choice of life (conditional on submission and defeat) or death (with honour for standing against the enemy).

What matters in any given situation depends on the circumstances of the moment, but for most people most of the time survival comes first. To survive we need air, so breathing matters. We need water, clean water, so drinking water matters. And we need food, so eating matters.

To live using only these things is the classic scenario of a hermit in Hindu or Buddhist lore, also of St Francis of Assisi, and others from various religious or philosophical schools. I've never attempted anything like that, but I did spend two weeks in solitude and total silence in 2004 as part of a month-long process of becoming a teacher, initially in a Tibetan Buddhist tradition. I had no books, music, radio, TV, news, or pen or paper. What I discovered was that it is not only possible to be happy with just food, water, clothing and shelter but that it was in fact incredible peaceful and content.

With mindfulness we can take this realisation, that we actually require very little in life, and use it deliberately to feel happy, calm, peaceful and fulfilled with the tiniest amount of things. It is the classic antidote to materialism, consumer impulses, and the often pointless hectic pace of life at which we blindly blunder through our days.

So some times in the day, preferably before you've worn yourself out, just stop and notice the vital signs that you're alive. The fact that you're thinking that fact is a sign. Notice that you can think. Feeling your feet on the floor, legs and back on the chair, air touching the skin on your hands and face, the cotton of your clothing on your shoulders and arms. Doing these things is inherently calming. It also in time makes you feel appreciative that you're alive and can experience these things. It de-stresses you and it takes nothing but a couple of minutes of your attention.

Or notice your breath, the most vital substance from outside our body that we need to stay alive. An in-breath, at the tips of the nostrils, is fresh, vibrant, even quite sharp to our mind. The outbreath in contrast is softer, more gentle and peaceful. Paying attention, especially a very light but clear attention, to the breath can bring to your mind that sense of being alert that the in-breath feels like, alongside the peaceful sense that an out-breath has. You can magnify the effect using words to yourself: Breathing in, my mind feels clear and alert; breathing out my mind is still, calm.

When you drink water – or coffee or tea but pure clear cold water is best as a mindfulness practice – feel the coolness of the water through the glass or cup on your fingertips, and just enjoy it. Just bring awareness of the very fact that you experience that sensation of coolness of touch. It's actually an astonishing feat of evolution over millions of years. Just note it.

Then feel the water on your lips; again, its coolness, and the pleasant feeling that sensation registers in your mind. Then in your mouth, cold and refreshing, lubrication the dryness of the mouth, cooling down its temperature.

When you eat, first notice that you have food available to you. If you are religious it is healthy to say Grace, to thank the entity you believe created everything including this bread and the opportunity for you to eat it. If atheist, just bring gratitude and appreciation to heart. And for all, perhaps put a little bit of your food to the side to eat at the very end, and imagine you have set it aside for one who has no food and needs it.

Happiness in being alive, peace in breathing, appreciation in water, and gratitude in the beauty of food on a plate. What more does a human being really need? My father broke his bread and shared it with his dying mother and his sisters.

What is a Healthy Mind?

According to some of the earliest Buddhist scriptures the Buddha once said to his followers

"There are two kinds of illnesses; physical illness and mental illness. There are people who enjoy freedom from physical illness all their lives. But it is rare in this world to find people who enjoy freedom from mental illness even for one moment…"

Which brings us to definitions. The Buddha wasn't talking about what we now consider mental illness. We think of schizophrenia and other forms of psychotic behaviour, possibly clinical depression or severe anxiety. But the Buddha was talking about what we consider supposedly normal people in their everyday situations.

He was talking about something far deeper and to my mind, more important. Consider this possibility; imagine you were really free from the habitual, instinctive, automatic, genetic and cultural negative or harmful programming and conditioning in your mind. You could potentially always be happy, full of love of life, considerate and understanding, kind and compassionate, fully engaged but not fanatical, gentle but strong, at peace but active in your life, grateful moment by moment just for the very fact of your existence – and still be a fully productive person in the community.

That's what the Buddha meant when he said we're all mentally ill. He was telling his followers that a completely mentally well person is one who has so worked on nurturing their mind that they have systematically flushed out and eradicated every single destructive and unhealthy thought, mood, emotion and feeling that automatically exists in them. Or at least they are so in control of their mind that they let such thoughts and feelings die away each and every time they arise, without these negative thoughts affecting the thinker or those around them. He was teaching that virtually no one has that degree of mental wellbeing; that instead most people are contaminated by unhelpful states of mind almost every moment of every day.

What an astonishing way of looking at mankind. Not just accepting the unpleasant and harmful thoughts that permeate our being. Rather that we could actually be completely liberated from all that junk and poison. Freed from all the pettiness that pops up in our mind, all the self-centred, prejudiced, judgemental views, and all the anger, bitterness, resentment, guilt and regrets about the past.

Even thinking about the possibility lightens the mind.

I believe this is possible, though I certainly don't pretend to be anywhere near it, as my wife and children will testify. However what is backed by an increasing amount of research by neuroscientists and doctors is that we can most definitely travel along that spectrum from a dysfunctional, often unhealthy automatic mind to one that is increasingly clear, calm, contented and kind-hearted. In my own work teaching mindfulness to all kinds of people amongst the general public here in Scotland and beyond people have told me they have ended years of insomnia, live much more purposefully even with severe depression, find beauty in mundane things when previously their mind only saw a jaded greyness in everything. One person said they stopped themselves right in the act of committing suicide, purely because of the qualities of mind that mindfulness nurtures.

It is only a matter of extrapolating this direction that people have been travelling on in terms of their mental wellbeing to see that if there was sufficient time, sufficient speed of improvement, and if the momentum of mental development can be sustained; that if those things were in place eventually a person might truly eliminate every last vestige of junk and harmful mental conditioning from their mind. Even if something in our genes means we can't get fully there, if you are moving to a progressively happier and clearer mind then the end point doesn't matter as you're just feeling better and better anyway.

What of death and divorce and suicides and crimes? What of Trump and Brexit and Indyref2 and petulant people on all sides pumping triumphalism or bile onto social media across the world? What of war in Syria and the plight of people in the four East African countries currently facing starvation? The Buddha considered that too in a famous phrase:

"How can there be joy or laughter when the world is ablaze?"

Then he answered it:

"Shrouded in darkness should you not seek light?"

He was referring to the world being ablaze as a result of human greed and anger and ignorance. Indeed he often referred to these destructive aspects of mind as fire because they burn everything around them leaving devastation both inside the mind that hosts them, and in the outside world that is affected by them.

But let's seek the light. When we feel inwardly strong, clear-headed, calm and happy despite the problems around us we are in a much better position to do something practical about things. Consider Nelson Mandela and Desmond Tutu as examples of forgiveness, contentment, and laughter even in the midst of turbulence.

So how can we got about nurturing our mental health using mindfulness?

Firstly always just stop. Pause. You are now mentally well, in that moment, just for that moment.

Now gently notice your breath as it flows in and out of your nostrils. You are mentally well as you do this.

Moreover you are, albeit in a tiny way, shifting the longer-term wellbeing of your mind in the direction of greater clarity, contentment, calmness and compassion.

Continue to do this regularly throughout your days and evenings and you will find yourself in much stronger mental shape in the long run. The Buddha said "With our thoughts we create the world", anticipating by 2,500 years the findings of neuroscience researchers, so if you want to be mentally fulfilled you have to start managing those thoughts!

Identity

Who are you? Let's consider it by letting me ask myself that question. Some of the words that appear to my mind are father, husband, mindfulness teacher, writer and poet, businessman, family history speaker.

These describe relationships or activities I do, with tangible evidence to back up my claims. I note that I no longer include the word Son in my list of who I am. My parents died three weeks apart in 2012. Maybe Orphan is the right word but I think of that as the word for a child, nor an adult.

Then the other, trickier words. Harder to pin down, to define.

Scot. European.

Not just tricky but inherently divisive, if by divisive we mean they cause the potential to say "them" and "us".

Not British. Though my passport says I am.

Not Irish – my mother's background - though other tests show that's part of my deep-seated roots (specifically Ulster despite my family tracing back to Wexford in the south-east of the Republic).

Nor Polish, even though I was privileged to receive a state honour last week from the country of my father's birth. DNA tests show me to be Eastern European, with a strong emphasis on the south-east region of Poland where Dad's family lived for centuries.

So I have no DNA-defined Scottishness in my body. Yet I thought "Scottish" when considering who I am in terms of national identity.

Then the wider words - Human, sentient living thing, part of the planet we call Earth, ultimately a very temporary aggregation of ever-changing sub-atomic particles in a vast universe, an aggregation that happens for now to experience something we call being alive.

This last list might seem to you to be a bit esoteric, left-field, even wishy-washy, though if you're reading a column on mindfulness you're probably more open-minded that that. It's the direction my mind has been moving in for the past twenty years since I first started practising mindfulness.

Interestingly this has not affected my political views or decisions made in the recent two referenda. This may simply show just how conditioned my political mind is, and that I haven't yet freed up my mind from narrow political and identity views. It has however changed dramatically how I engage in political discussion, especially around the man-made notions of national or indeed supra-national identity.
I am now very aware that much scientific research has shown that political views, especially those related to authoritarianism or liberalism on the one hand, and elitism or egalitarianism on the other, are genetic. In other words, we are born prone to have certain political or socio-economic views. Life experiences then reinforce or modify these.

So my supposedly reasoned and deeply considered reflections on politics are actually to a greater or lesser extent, the views rubber-stamped on the genes my mum and dad bequeathed to me not even at birth, but nine months before then. So instead of the midwife saying "It's a boy Mrs. Stepek" (to which my mum would have answered, not another one!) she should have said "It's a Green-leaning liberal Mrs. Stepek". But national identity is not genetic; it is an accident of where you were born or how people around you influenced your views on the subject. In other words it is artificial but extremely powerful.

Things do shift however, especially when you deliberately cultivate your mind through practices like mindfulness. When you repeatedly see the same manmade senses of identity arising in your head, and when you realise these are just forms of cultural conditioning, you also see that they block you from being a wider and deeper type of person. You see not only yourself but others from a conditioned ie. prejudiced view. The prejudice might be positive. When I worked my way round the world in my youth I always loved bumping into fellow Scots, even before I worked out what they were like as people. It might be positive but it was still prejudging them.

This is not actually that relevant to the major issues of the day, Brexit and Indyref too, though some of the readers who are conditioned in any of these matters might think I am making a political case. I'm not.

One can see the inherent human or mental problem in identifying as Scottish, British, or European yet still reason that an independent Scotland is the best governance structure for Scotland. Or that it would be better to remain as the U.K. Similarly if we extend the political landscape to membership of the E.U. A case can be made for any of the four options In-in, in-out, out-in or out-out, and this does not need to depend on any form of identity at all.

But for me personally I am now more concerned that we as a species still do not think or act from a whole planet or universal perspective. This big picture view is skewed by narrower identification with nation or political entity. We have climate change, multiple wars, horrific inequality (in which most Scots count as the mega-rich), and a destructive form of economics in my view. If we primarily focus on Scottish, British or European issues then we don't actually deal with the bigger issues that cause the most suffering and heartache. So look deeply with mindfulness at how you define yourself, and see if there are aspects which you feel may be blocking your potential to be fully yourself.

Being Reborn

It's Easter Sunday, the most important date in the Christian religion. Whilst the percentage of people in Scotland who say they follow a particular religion has dropped, including the number of Christians, and the numbers attending regular church services has declined even more rapidly, still most Scots have some cultural heritage in this religion. Moreover many people while not identifying themselves with a particular religion or church, do have a sense of spirituality, or a wider belief that something bigger than us is present.

This is not something I personally experience, nor do I follow any faith. But whether we consider ourselves religious, spiritual, or neither, the annual festive date of the Resurrection of Jesus from the dead, as written in the New Testament, can give us pause to reflect on our own lives.

Leaving aside the core issue that divides people – Jesus as God or Jesus as just another human, albeit hugely influential – it is useful to remember the back story leading up to the Resurrection. Here is a man, a radical teacher, sometimes abrupt, impatient, but with views that remain astonishing, at least in my opinion. He has in the space of a few short years gathered an immense following, with crowds flocking to his talks.

His popularity and his pointed disagreement with the traditional mainstream views of the time, make him a feared enemy of many influential people.

They plot his downfall and the Roman overseers wash their hands of the matter. He is then tortured, humiliated publicly, abused then left to die in a deliberately agonisingly slow and cruel way, nailed or tied to a cross of wood. It is an utterly appalling scene, this young man in his early thirties, brave and earnest in his teachings, made to die an excruciatingly painful death.

Then of course possibly the most controversial moment in human history. The stories in the four gospels say he rose from the dead three days after his death.

How does this relate to our own lives?

Interestingly five hundred years before Jesus's time one of the other great founders of what we consider nowadays a religion, The Buddha, was also talking about death and resurrection. He came from the traditions of his own time, part of which was the doctrine of rebirth or reincarnation. This proposed that although we die, something continues in another form of life, a life that could be of an animal, bird, insect, or indeed a God or a creature of hellish proportions. Your future form of rebirth depended on your actions in your previous lives and current life.

The Buddha changed two things about this belief. Firstly, and radically, he proposed that it was our mental intentions that cause future effects, rather than the actions themselves.

As an example, suppose you accidentally kill someone in a road accident through no fault of your own. In the Buddha's time it was believed that this would result in future negative consequences for you, but for the Buddha, as there was no intent to harm, there would be no future negative effects.

Likewise, if you had the intention to kill someone but never carried it out, the traditional view would be that as there was no action, there would be no consequences, whereas for the Buddha the intention itself would lead to future negative effects.

But more importantly the Buddha was ambivalent about rebirth. Although there are numerous stories about his altruism in past lives, in many of his talks he specifically refuses to talk of what happens after we die, suggesting it was an area of speculation which was not useful to explore as it was not knowable. This was more typical of his reasoning method than the tales of past lives.

More interesting for our own lives is that he postulated the remarkable statement that we die and are reborn in every moment. This reminds me of Bob Dylan's beautiful lyrics "he not busy being born is busy dying". The idea is that we have opportunity in each moment. Once that moment goes the opportunity is lost. It is dead and gone. But lo and behold another moment appears. Another opportunity.

An opportunity in mindfulness terms to notice what's actually going on in that moment, whether through our senses – what do we see, hear, touch, smell, taste – or what is on our minds in terms of thoughts and automatic reactions to what's going on.

If we unconsciously just flow with the automatic unconscious reactions of the mind we are essentially dead to the moment. We have not brought our deliberate, clearer and more considerate qualities to bear on the situation. A Harvard study showed that we are like this a whopping 47% of our waking moments. Just short of half of our lives are lost – effectively dead or at least zombie-like – through unawareness.

Now think of someone you love who has died. Or if no one close to you has passed away, think of a hero from the past who is long gone. I think of Marie Curie, or Maria Sklodowska-Curie to give her proper name. What would your loved one or hero give to experience just a few moments like the ones we have, the ones we so neglectfully let slip through absence of mere attention.

So on this Easter day rise from the dead of wasteful autopilot living, and experience the miracle of being alive, and of the life around you, in the people, the pets, the animals and bird, plants, clouds, sunshine or rain.
Good Books

It's World Book Day today so I'd like to discuss some of my favourite books as they relate to the practice and understanding of mindfulness.

Books can be a problem for people who want to learn mindfulness, and I've found this to be especially the case amongst Scottish people. Hopefully without generalising too much Scots can be a bit too intellectual in their pursuit of truth, beauty and the other big things in life. And learning a lot about something is not the same as learn in order to practice something. In fact it's just like the inverse correlation between sales of cook books – rising - and amount of cooking being done – falling. Often people use reading about a subject as an unconscious excuse not to practice.

Moreover I have seen a trend repeatedly over the last twenty years of people who want to try whatever is the next new thing, especially if it has and doctors have shown that it works at a mental health and physical brain level.

So to books. Read to understand mindfulness, and read to analyse the scientific evidence to reassure yourself that you're not falling for yet another shallow fad. University of Oxford Professor of Clinical Psychology Mark Williams and Danny Penman's co-authored book Mindfulness: A Practical Guide to Finding Peace in a Frantic World is in my view the best overall general text on mindfulness, full of the science behind it, but also what it entails, and how to do it. And it has a really handy free CD of eight audio recordings of practices so you can be guided by them at home.

There are many other mindfulness books including by pioneering researchers such as Doctor Jon Kabat-Zinn and neuroscientist Richard Davidson but stick to one book and re-read it several times to let it all sink in deeply. Other good general guides that are less highbrow than Mark Williams' one include Ken Verni's Practical Mindfulness: A Step by Step Guide, a beautiful book to look at as well as easy to read, and a little gem called Mindfulness on the Go by the American paediatrician Jan Chozen Bays who combines her medical career with being the abbess of a Zen monastery in Oregon. This little book, which can fit into the pocket of a pair of jeans, has twenty-five simple practices that those who live in the Zen centre do in a daily rotation.

Now to the really deep stuff if you're interested. Two books on Buddhism have been great friends to me for the past twenty years or so. What the Buddha Taught by Sri Lankan monk Walpola Sri Rahula is generally recognised as the finest explanation of what this remarkable man taught 2,500 years ago. Alongside the mindfulness practices that the Buddha developed for the benefit of himself and others, Rahula explains the Buddha's truly wise and still relevant advice on everything from financial matters, ethical entrepreneurship, family relationships and of course the all-pervasive nature of the unreliable, volatile minds we have. I must have read this book fifty times or more.

The Dhammapada is a collection of sayings of the Buddha, compiled some centuries after the Buddha lived but still before the time of Jesus. It is full of teachings that still have the power to make us think. The very first lines are: "All our experiences are preceded by mind, led by mind, created by mind." This is a fundamental truth which we still struggle to understand.

Alongside these truly great works are the two classics of American philosopher and naturalist Henry David Thoreau. His Walden is the greatest hymn to nature and simple living ever written, whilst his speech-turned-essay called Civil Disobedience inspired everyone from Tolstoy to Gandhi to Martin Luther King. This is applied mindfulness in action, and the two books can change your life dramatically.

Finally it would be falsely modest of me not to mention my own volumes of writings on Mindful Living. They aim to help people see how to apply mindfulness in everyday real life situations. People have been kind enough to say they carry the books with them in their handbags or have them at their bedside cabinet to read before going to bed.

But remember above all else. Practice, practice, practice. Reading should be a stimulus to do the work, not a sneaky way of avoid it.

Enjoying Chores

What's your most loathed household task? There's so much to choose from but from a straw poll of friends over the years, ironing seems to win this dubious honour. Of course there's so many more possible choices of things we have to do but hate doing. Washing the dishes, putting them away, hoovering, sweeping and mopping the floor, giving your kids a lift, picking them back up afterwards, cutting the grass, emptying the bins. Our life is full of what we consider menial tasks, to be endured as necessary evils.

The human mind is easily irritated. In contrast a month or so ago my wife and I spotted a female blackbird in our garden one day gathering straw and bits of grass to make a nest. We watched it carefully and saw exactly where the nest was, in our back garden beside the neighbour's garage.

She had spent hours of work constructing it. Her male partner was always perched on a nearby higher branch, presumably watching out for potential attacks on his partner. A few days later for some unknown reason she felt she had to abandon the nest.

Later that same week we saw her again, straw in her mouth, this time going into thick vines at the side of our front garden. Same process; days of hard work, her partner up high ensuring the couple and their future offspring would be as safe as possible. Finally it was complete and they're still happily there.

Can you imagine a human response to having to redo a task like that? Moaning about the fact of the double amount of work. Probably bemoaning that all the best materials had now been used up. Blaming each other for the fact that the first nest wasn't safe enough. Blaming each other for not doing enough work. Cursing fate for how hard their lives had turned out to be.

It's a simple thing to say that if a task has to be done just go and do it and stop whinging about it. It's a lot harder to do in practice. Our minds are programmed to moan, to get annoyed at trivial things, to try to pin the blame on someone else for anything untoward that happens. In the animal kingdom we are the champion moaning-faced gits.

But it's not our fault, or rather it's our mind's fault. Asked if you would choose to complain or moan about everyday chores most people would say no, and yet that's what most of us do. It's an automatic reaction, made into a habit by sheer scale of repetition over years if not decades.

The problem with this is that every time we automatically react like this we strengthen the habit, making it even more likely that we'll react the same way in future. It's the classic vicious circle. And lest you think that it's no big deal, consider the fact that the more your mind gets used to moaning or complaining about little everyday things, the more likely it is to spread to other matters too. This is how us males slowly evolve into grumpy old men (and I'd suggest women are not immune to it either).

Moreover, mindfulness reminds us forcefully that we can only experience the wonder of being alive in the present moment, the fleeting passage of a brief snippet of time. If we spend precious moments moaning these are wasted, and wasted forever. We can't retrieve them. We don't get a second crack at those moments. Finally, they run out. No more moments.

So what should we do about ironing, washing dishes, cutting the grass? Just notice the physical activity itself. The left-right repetitive motion of the iron over the clothes, the skill of the hand-eye coordination that means you can do this fairly effortlessly, perhaps even in time the sheer peaceful – even enjoyable – feeling in your mind when you are actually undertaking a simple task. In other words being mindful of chores can literally become simultaneously relaxing and nurturing. Paying attention to the actual task itself means you are exercising the mental skill of mindfulness. This brings you mental health benefits, sharpens your intellect, and even makes you a more bearable person to those around you, all while you are just mopping the floor.

Life feels precious when you see that it is not infinite. One day you won't be able to experience what it is like to notice an iron gliding skilfully over a cotton tee shirt and making its creases smooth. As Joni Mitchell put it "You don't know what you've got till it's gone". Mindfulness demands that right here, right now – you do know what you've got. Notice it. Appreciate it. Love it. Be grateful that you have it. Thank luck, fate, chance, God or whatever that you have it. Appreciate your life even when you are cleaning out the toilet bowl.

The more you notice, without inner commentary, without moaning, the more you come to love your life. Life itself. The very realisation of being alive in a moment. And when the moans come up, as they will, don't get annoyed at your mind, because getting annoyed is just creating another moan. Don't suppress it either because this causes the feeling to return strengthened. Instead just gently let it fade away, by focussing on the breath, or back to the task. Then just enjoy your work.

Stop Worrying

There's an old parable in the Chinese classic, The Book of Chuang Tzu. Two poor farmers are neighbours, one old and wise, the other younger. One day the old farmer's only horse escaped and ran away. The neighbour said "What a shame" but the old man replied "Who knows how things work out in life?" and seemed unperturbed.

The next day the horse came back, and following it, five other horses, which the old farmer trapped in his fence. The neighbour laughed and said "How lucky you are!" and the old man replied much the same as before "Who knows how things turn out in this life?"

A few days later the old man's son tried to tame one of the horses but it reared up and brought its leg right onto the son's thigh, breaking the bone. When the neighbour heard he came round and consoled the old man "That's terrible, I hope he recovers soon." You can by now guess the old man's reply.

Finally, a week or so later a section of the Imperial Chinese Army turned up in the area. They had a new campaign and were forcing all the local young men to join up and fight for them. When they saw that the old farmer's son was in bed with a broken leg they didn't take him away.

The neighbour was so pleased for the old man and his son. "That was such a lucky thing!" and of course the old man just repeated himself "Who knows how things might turn out in this strange life?"

That story dates from the last half of the fourth century BC yet its message is timeless. People get caught up in the suffering of a moment's bad luck. We get things way out of proportion, and even when things look terribly bleak, we simply don't know how things might turn out.

My family story is a perfect example. My dad, born in Poland, was forced into a Soviet labour camp at the age of seventeen. His mother died of hunger, his father of cancer in the Resistance, he lost his home, the small farm he was to inherit, and the part of Poland he was born and raised in was annexed by Stalin who now ran all of Poland. So he had nowhere to go. All seemed unbearably dark in his life.

But within a decade he was at the start of a hugely successful business life in Scotland, and he lived a full, rich, and giving life till he died at the age of ninety. Who know how things turn out in life after all?

So how do we get from being in the younger farmer's position – flitting between naïve hopes and speculative despair – to having a mind like the wise old man in the story. In these times, between Brexit and the U.S. Election result we surely need more than ever a clear and calm mind, a mind that doesn't allow knee-jerk reactions to weigh us down, a mind that assesses the situation in reality not through endless conjectures?

Mindfulness trains our mind to do just this. And should you react immediately with a cynical sneer, or even a sceptical doubt, note that the following is from the NHS's own site on the subject, quoting Professor Mark Williams, Emeritus Professor of Psychology at the University of Oxford.

"Mindfulness also allows us to become more aware of the stream of thoughts and feelings that we experience," says Professor Williams, "and to see how we can become entangled in that stream in ways that are not helpful.

"This lets us stand back from our thoughts and start to see their patterns. Gradually, we can train ourselves to notice when our thoughts are taking over and realise that thoughts are simply 'mental events' that do not have to control us.

"Most of us have issues that we find hard to let go and mindfulness can help us deal with them more productively. We can ask: 'Is trying to solve this by brooding about it helpful, or am I just getting caught up in my thoughts?'

"Awareness of this kind also helps us notice signs of stress or anxiety earlier and helps us deal with them better."

So try it. Now if possible. Just for two minutes as a trial. Read the instructions below then give it a go.

Sitting comfortably, gently close your eyes so what you see doesn't become a distraction.

Now allow your mind, your attention, to loosen, to lighten, so that it feels weightless, effortless but all the clearer because it is now very light and relaxed.

Notice your breath with this clear but very light attention. Note that the in-breath may feel quite cool, fresh, and enlivening, very pleasant.

In contrast note that the out-breath is like a warm, measure release of pressure, like a valve just opened a little. Note that this feels peaceful to the mind.

Try not to use words to describe your experience. Rather, see if you can soak into the raw, unadorned feel of the air flowing in and out through your nostrils.

To nurture good qualities of mind you can use word association. As you breathe in you can slowly think "breathing in, my mind is clear" then "breathing out, my mind feels peaceful".

Do this just for a minute or two then very slowly and gently allow your eyes to open slowly.

Not Meditation

I really don't like the word meditation. It makes lots of intelligent people run a mile thinking "new age rubbish" or "hippy nonsense". Not exactly a word that convinces people to give it a try then, is it?

Actually the word is a very poor translation of bhavana (rhymes with banana) in Pali, an ancient Indian tongue. It meant mental culture or cultivation. In other words deliberate development of the mind. And that's what the very fashionable thing known as "mindfulness meditation" is, a tool to develop the mind just like gym equipment are tools to develop the body, and a university is an institution to develop knowledge and skills.

And if you're just about to dismiss that explanation with a cynical, maybe arrogant mind, then have a quick look at who says mindfulness works. You just might find they are a lot more qualified than you to assess it, unless of course you are one of those up and coming post-truth, post-expert types who are now all the rage in certain parts of the UK, USA, France and Austria amongst other countries.

Oxford University has a Centre for Mindfulness. Its research showed that practising mindfulness can reduce a person's chances of getting another bout of depression by 60% if they have a pattern of recurrent depression. Given that there around one in seven Scots are on antidepressants right now, that's suddenly a very important thing.

Imagine the difference it can make to a single individual who has suffered recurring depression to feel they are free from it, and have a simple tool to help them stay clear of it.

Harvard University teach it in their business degrees because mindfulness has been shown to improve attention, sustain focus, improve cognitive decision-making. It also nurtures our sense of compassion for others, something one would hope is high up on the list of current and future business leaders.

It's how I got to know about mindfulness, co-owning and running a business. Stepek. It's not a name you can hide behind in Scotland. It's not Smith or McDonald. We're the only family of that surname in the country, so if you're advertise on TV, radio and the press thirty times a month for twenty years, alongside our co-conspirators, Glens, Hutchison and Robertson, then pretty soon you find you've become a household name in the Central Belt.

Running a business proved to be enjoyable much to my surprise but combining it with family issues – we were a big family business, with my nine siblings all co-owners and more than half of us working in the business – proved stressful. So by a combination of luck, chance, and a bit of searching one day I found myself with a book in my hands, Buddhism: Plain and Simple by an American, Steve Hagen. He was a Zen priest. I was sceptical. I'm still a natural sceptic.

I promised myself that I'd intellectually tear to shreds all the religious and philosophical points I assumed the book would describe, then hand the book into a charity shop next time I was passing. Except that didn't happen. I found that Hagen's explanation of what the Buddha taught was pretty devoid of dogma, very modern and psychoanalytical in tone, and made a huge amount of sense to me about how to try and cope and flourish in the modern world. Not bad for a guy who lived in 500BC.

At the heart of his teachings was this thing called Mindfulness. It's about noticing what's actually going on in the present moment, something we are not good at as a species. We are easily distracted. In fact we are distracted an average of 46.9% of the time, day in, day out, according to Harvard. That's not exactly a high standard of paying attention. So mindfulness is the pure, raw unadorned noticing of what we might see, hear, touch, taste, smell or perceive in our mind at any given time… all the time… every single moment if we can do it. That means it's not really a thing we do every so often, like football or watching Strictly; it's a way of being, because we're supposed to be doing it all the time, moment by moment.

That's not easy to achieve but it is doable to a greater or lesser degree. It takes practice and that where unsatisfying word "meditation" comes back into the equation. If you want to be a good tennis player you have to train. It doesn't come just by playing lots of games. Same with the mind. If you want to be able to notice more clearly, more objectively, more insightfully, you need to do the preparatory work.

It's worth it. The more than six thousand academic papers on the benefits of mindfulness show reductions not only in depression but stress, worry, low self-esteem; greater resistance to infections, lower blood pressure; better intellectual results in schools and colleges; and the remarkable growth in kindness and compassion towards others. In short you nurture Clarity, Calmness, Contentment, and Kindness.

So what's the training like. You can do it now if you like. Just sitting where you are, notice what your body feels like sitting on your chair. Maybe the softness of the couch, the firmness of the kitchen chair, or if you're standing the feel of your feet on the ground. That feeling is what we mean by being well grounded. We're in touch with raw reality, our heads are not lost in our concerns. This is being mindful. Do it.

Resolve to Have no More Resolutions

Ah it's that time of year again. The post-New Year Resolution feeling of guilt and self-criticism. Or – and apologies for my pessimism but the stats back me up – if you're still pushing through with your resolution there's a 90% chance it'll lapse by the end of the month. So no three cheers for resolutions.

Mindfulness asks us to notice things as they actually are, moment by moment. When we do this with regards to resolutions we notice that they generally don't do the job we ask of them. Worse, they make us feel miserable for failing. With mindfulness we can notice that will power, well it lacks power. The will is there but there's no juice in the engine. The engine is the mind. Your mind. So there's the problem. It's almost always the problem and that why mindfulness focusses so much of its attention on our thoughts and feelings.

This is strange. It's your mind that wants to lose ten pounds but it's the same mind that wants to stuff your face with scones and leftover chocolates from Christmas. Talk about the enemy within.

Actually it's two distinct areas of the brain at work (though that's technically a wee bit simplistic because most of the brain is used to a greater or lesser extent most of the time but my point is correct in general terms).

One area deals with reasoning, decision-making, clear thinking; the other ignites fight or flight responses. Think of the Numbskulls and imagine you have Mr. Spock in one corner and Dick Dastardly from Wacky Races in the other. This is what we have to contend with in our everyday inner life.

Every time Mr. Spock proudly decides he'll have you resolve to give up smoking, alcohol, cakes, whatever it's just a matter of time before Dick Dastardly plots to stop you on the road to success. And unlike in the cartoons, he generally succeeds. So you need to neutralise his plans.

I gave up drinking alcohol around the year 2000. I didn't drink a lot but I disliked the occasional hangover I felt, and I hated the loss of a half day that this caused. I didn't make a resolution at all. I just treated it as an experiment of my then early days practising mindfulness. Each time the desire for a beer or red wine popped into my mind I noticed it for what it was – just something that pops up from time to time . This is the core skill of mindfulness - to recognise that this is all it is, just something that the mind creates. Our task as people who want sane, happy lives, is to discern whether it's Mr. Spock giving us clear thought-through advice, or if it's Dastardly throwing TNT on the road in front of us. Thanks to my mindfulness I was able to give up instantly and have never lapsed. No resolution, not even a determination to stop drinking. I just stopped and never restarted.

Through the week ahead try to notice whenever a want pops up into your head.

You might call it a craving, a desire, a yearning, a need. It's when your mind tells you that you are dissatisfied because right now you lack something, and you can only be satisfied if you get the drink, food, love, pat on the head, or whatever it is your mind tells you you want.

Note it down on your phone if you have a Notes section, or in a private journal. You don't need to try to block the craving though you can if you want to, and should if you're under doctor's orders. What matters for now is gaining familiarity with what your brain comes up with.

This isn't as easy as it sounds. We are so used to things popping up in our mind that we don't usually even notice that this is in fact what's happening. Rather we just do what our mind says without question. We know this as being on autopilot. So you'll miss a heap of these wants when they arise. Don't bother about that. Bothering about it is just a waste of your time. Simply try to notice the next one; believe me, it won't be long in coming.

If you do get annoyed that you've missed several wants, note your annoyance in your journal or phone. Annoyance is itself another mental creation signifying that you wanted something but didn't get it; so it's another desire made by your mind. Complicated isn't it? Frustrating too; and this is the thing that runs your life day to day.

Keep up the note taking. After a couple of days you'll start to see the same stuff arising.

Then you can stop writing the actual desire down and just make a stroke or an asterisk alongside your previous note each time the same thought arises. Doing this exercise – which I still do from time to time almost twenty years after I first did it - you'll learn a few key life lessons. You'll see for real the extent of the habitual, automatic, recurring nature of most of our thoughts; and you can compare the relative frequency of each.

Just notice. No vows. The familiarity you gain will itself act as a kind of gentle distancing of you and your thoughts. Basically Spock is getting a bit more in charge. Just keep practising.

Mindfulness in Society

With local elections just passed and the snap General Election around the corner I thought it might be interesting to explore where mindfulness could fit in a positive manifesto for society.

Whilst a very robust and extensive amount of research shows that virtually everyone can derive great benefits from mindfulness, there are groups who I feel are priorities or who would benefit most.

Let's start with school teachers and the senior management and others in our primary and secondary schools. Teachers are amongst the most stressed and fatigued people in the country. Their role is indisputably of the greatest importance, yet they get little recognition for what they do.

All teachers should be trained deeply in mindfulness so that they can manage the stress and irritations that come with the job. There should be a systematic programme rolled out to achieve this, and all trainee teachers qualify as mindfulness teachers as part of their teacher training.

Whilst we train the teachers in mindfulness we should, at the same time bring regular mindfulness sessions to all pupils of primary and secondary schools. Classes could be started and ended with two minutes of silent practice, whilst a deeper understanding of the neuroscience and workings of the mind can be systematically worked into the school curriculum.

This would equip children for the challenges of adolescence, the cultural pressures towards alcohol, cigarettes, and drugs, and nurture compassion, friendships, tolerance and mature sexual behaviour. As a scientific-based subject mindfulness can readily fit within secular or faith school systems. Such a strategy could be transformative and liberating for the teaching profession and pupils, bringing a much gentler and kindly culture to schools, and, as the evidence shows, raising intellectual attainment.

I'd love to see parents and their children being taught mindfulness together, as happens in my Hamilton class, where often couples come to the class together, sometimes with their children, occasionally three generations together. This nurtures a common language and understanding within the home, and helps bond families.

The other area I'd like to see mindfulness introduced into a whole area of society is criminal justice, especially prisons. I believe that much of how our life unfolds is purely by chance. Some are lucky, some unlucky. We can be lucky with the genes we inherit, the parents we had. Lucky with all sorts of things as we grow up – a special teacher, good local facilities, a chance meeting. Others are unlucky in life - their genes, their parents, the events that shape who they become. Some of those people are now in prison.

Prison is extraordinarily expensive. Moreover rehabilitation of offenders isn't particularly successful. Reoffending rates are high.

Prisoners could be trained in how their minds work, how they came to do the crimes that they are in prison for, how to manage their lives while imprisoned, and how to shape the content and culture of their minds in readiness for life back in society. I have done several mindfulness talks and sessions in prisons in Scotland, for staff and inmates. Amongst many there is a deep sense that such training, properly introduced and integrated into the daily rituals of the prison system, would help change the culture in each institution and prepare staff and inmates alike for the present moment and the future.

There is a connection between the prison system and schools of course. Some children have one or both parents in prison. Clearly therefore many prisoners are parents. The children of people in prison need help in coping with so many aspects of their lives; and if they knew that their mother or father was learning mindfulness at the same time as the children themselves were learning it at school, the potential for mutual support and a renewed relationship would multiply.

Victims of crime – and often their family members - need mindfulness for an entirely different reason, and can be considered as having similar needs to those who have suffered other forms of trauma. These include people who have served in the horrors of war, people who have experienced or witnessed terrible injuries, and most poignantly of all, people whose family members or closest friends have committed suicide.

When you consider all of these groups put together we can see that, underneath the thin sheen of normality in our society there is a very large group of people who live with very deeply ingrained pain, grief, anger and other forms of mental suffering.

What these people have in common is that the tragic suffering continues long after the cause of the suffering occurred. In some cases, especially murder, rape or suicide, the individuals generally fight the very idea of moving on, because to do suggests to the human mind that the perpetrator in some way gets off the hook, or that to move on would be disloyal or even an abandonment of the loved one they are grieving for. And yet the suffering they endure is so debilitating.

There is substantial evidence that many people who suffer from trauma of these kinds may benefit significantly from practising mindfulness.

So in my mindfulness mini-manifesto we could use the practices to help teachers, schools, pupils, prisoners, prison staff, and those suffering from trauma to live happier, healthier, more resilient and more joyful lives. Properly thought through this could be delivered at extremely modest costs. Ah well, now it's in the hands of the politicians.

Living with the Enemy Within

Einstein said "Common sense is the collection of prejudices acquired by age eighteen".

Unfortunately some of these prejudices are very difficult to dislodge, even when we know intellectually and culturally that they are unacceptable, even obnoxious. People of my generation – I'm 58 – were raised in a culture that was racist. Not in the way that we know racism today. The racism I grew up in was explicit. There were very few black people in Scotland, none in Hamilton to my recollection in the 1960s. But there was a derogatory word for every nationality people could think of. Spanish, Italian, Pakistani people all had short negative names.

Homosexuality was illegal. At Scotland v England football games Scottish football fans sang "We hate Jimmy Hill, he's a ..." with the last word being an unpleasant slang word for a gay person. Those watching the game on television, laughed when that song was sung, as they did when the same fans sung "If you hate the fu**ing English clap your hands".

Let's not go any further. It's quite unsettling to realise how much our own culture conditions us so insidiously. I can't remember a single person telling me to think in negative ways about different people, and yet these views soaked into me like an invisible poison.

This is how the brain learns. It's not just unpleasant things that soak in by a form of mental osmosis. I was taught to be considerate of others, not to be greedy, and other ethical behaviours, and hopefully many of those have stuck with me.

The problem as I see it, is not so much that some of our conditioned thinking is harmful or hurtful to ourselves or others, but that none of it was freely chosen by us. It was all something that happened to us.

In neuroscience this is called neuroplasticity. Plastic originally meant the ability to be shaped. So the material we call plastic is so-called because when warmed up it becomes softer and more malleable, making it easy to shape into different products or parts. In recent decades the scientists of the mind, the neuroscientists, have been able to detect that who we are – i.e. our thoughts, personality, traits, opinions – is constantly being affected moment by moment by our experiences. Over time those experiences coalesce into habitual ways of judging the world or anything around us.

Or they reinforce existing ways of perceiving things. Sometimes an experience can be so extraordinary or radical that it can jolt us entirely out our old ways of thinking and create a new way of seeing ourselves, others, or the world. Many examples of these are unfortunately negative, often surrounding tragedy. We call some examples trauma, and the lasting-effects of these experiences, post-traumatic stress disorder or PTSD.

The classic example is of soldiers returning from war, but families of murder victims, domestic abuse, and family suicides usually result in some major changes to how we see life.

The typical way we perceive these people is that they are in some way entirely different from us. We are normal; they are not. But it's not quite as black and white as that. It's more like a spectrum where sufferers from PTSD and similar traumatic experiences are at one pole, and nearly all of us are somewhere closer to the middle of the line, or indeed beyond that, moving towards the more than average levels of happiness and joy.

However one thing every one of us has in common is that where we are on that spectrum is because of life experiences, aided by the genes we got from our ancestors.

Mindfulness helps us see that this is the case, not theoretically, nor solely in words, but through experience of observing it in ourselves in real time. So, for example, when I watch the news mindfully I become instantly aware of my prejudices, favourable or unfavourable, towards any politician who appears. Some of my prejudices are really ugly and hateful. With my mindfulness I notice them and allow them to fall away, giving me a calmer, more objective view of what the politician is saying. I don't mean that my political opinion is necessarily unthinking or unreasoned, just that I have become so attached to it that I exaggerate or inflate my views on the people who don't hold the same views as me.

My daily mindfulness practices, whether the quiet solitary ones at the start or end of day, or mini-ones sprinkled through the day, in addition to my attempts to notice without judgement what's actually going on moment by moment, these all add up to a type of self-defence against the worst extremes that have been lodged in my mind through my lifetime. They also act as a slow but sure method of combating and withering those prejudices and harmful emotional reactions I still have; and believe me I have plenty to deal with.

It's not just thoughts or views that can be lodged deeply in your mindset. Stress, anxiety, depression, self-loathing. These too are formed from life experiences and become habitual states of mind that haunt you, seemingly at random. At a more minor level frequent irritations, frustration, annoyance, impatience also become part of who we are. Mindfulness can help us firstly see these for what they are – just mental habits created by experiences. Then it can help you cope with, manage, and finally neutralise them. Over time you can start to be in control over who you are and how you think.

Elite without Elitism

At the very pinnacle of sport it's got nothing to do with technique, fitness, strength. Everyone's got all of that. That's why they're the ones vying for the number one spot. Think of Andy Murray, Serena Williams or Novak Djokovic in tennis. They've all been number one in the world but at moments, not through injury or a drop in skills or strength, they've dropped down the rankings, or simply lost games they were expected to easily win.

At the elite level in sport it is mostly a mental game. The one with the clearest, most readied and prepared focus wins the day. The focus is literally moment by moment. Imagine being on a tennis court, two sets to love down, five-four down in the third set, and forty-love against you, meaning that your opponent has three chances to serve to win the whole match. What mental strength, control, clarity does it takes to drop all thoughts of defeats from your mind. What mental power does it take to not even think about the very facts of your present situation, that even if you win the point, you have to face another two chances of losing the match.

And even if you win the game, you have to go through it all again, game after game. And if you win the set you're still two sets to love down. Most of us would just give in. Some of would already have lost our temper at ourselves for making unforced errors, and our mind would be ruminating over points too easily lost, all of which distracts us from the next ball coming our way.

The control over their mind at such moments is pure mindfulness. Don't be distracted from what you want to do in the next single moment. Don't project into an imagined future where you'll win the point, or lose it. Don't allow your mind to look back with annoyance or regret. Simply be, fully, clearly, in the fleeting point of reality we call the moment.

Then do the same with the next moment. Then the next. And so on until the match ends.

That may sound like a horrible way to actually live your life or as a career, though of course at that level there's a huge financial reward for those who reach the top. But can we use mindfulness to take the best of elite's sport's mental discipline without the arduous aspects of their job?

Instead of managing the mind in order to win glory, we can bring increasing control over the mind to live a fulfilled, joyful and compassionate life. Instead of fears about a significant moment in a sport, imagine we are able to let go of negative thoughts about a minor situation or a bad memory from the past.

Imagine moment by moment you can assess whether the content arising in your mind is helpful or unhelpful, nurturing or destructive, and in that moment drop what harms or wastes, and make the most of what feels good or right, not just for you but for all around you.

This is doable, and if you continue the practices of mindfulness that let you do it, you can bring increasing degrees of stability and enjoyment of life. As you develop this skill I think it is accurate to say you can move to a comparison with the elites in sport. Can you become elite as living your life? Not for that spurious word success or material gain, but for the sheer beauty of experiencing more and more richly what it is to live this thing we call life?

Just notice your breath gently flowing in at the tip of your nostrils. The sensation you feel is unique to this moment. Unique to you. Others will have their own sensations. The mere fact that you can experience awareness of the feelings is a remarkable confirmation of being alive. Moreover it is for most people most of the time a very pleasant, enlivening and peaceful experience to your mind.

If from the feeling you can gain a sense of how precious your life is, then you can allow that insight to soak into your conscious mind, let it linger, let it become part of how you may think in the future. From this comes, slowly but surely, appreciation as an ever-present factor of your everyday life. And from appreciation comes gratitude for the lucky chance that you have a life to experience, or if you are religious, to thank God or whatever other creator you believe gave you life. In addition, as you come to appreciate the everyday moments of being alive in a very clear, calm and stable way, you come to notice those who are still suffering, and compassion develops in response.

To my mind this is elite living. Noticing the actual experiences of being alive moment by moment, with a heightened awareness and clarity of thought. Appreciating all your experience, feeling grateful for the opportunity to experience these changing moments. And giving to those who need help. I think that is a greater definition of elite performance than winning Wimbledon or the World Cup or Champions League. It is elite living without elitism. It is the joy of life, achieved through moment by moment mindfulness, and the letting go of any junk the mind creates, allowing us instead to create beauty out of ugliness, calmness out of anger, and joy out of despair.

Reasons to be Cheerful

I'm currently reading a book on how people become politically reactionary. It's by an American author. I'm not enjoying it much but what interests me is his view that many people have a tendency to hanker back to "the good old days" or a golden age in their country's history. We see this in the USA and UK political spheres, with phrases such as "Let's take back control" and "Make America great again". Both phrases suggest how much better things used to be, and by inference how bad things are now.

We also see it in people's views about everyday things like music, football, and television programmes. All those great bands and singers – how I miss Bob Marley! - those brilliant teams we used to have, when "real footballers" showed how the beautiful game should be played, and the brilliant television programmes of the 1960s or 70s. It seems we have on the one hand, a built-in nostalgia, and on the other a pessimistic view of the present and future.

Obviously sometimes that perspective would be accurate. Compare my father's life in 1938 with five years' later in 1943. In 1938 we had just left school and was an agricultural student in a secure, loving farming household, not very well-off, but living a good life. Five years later his mother was dead, from starvation, his father dead from cancer, his home destroyed, his country occupied by Stalinists and Nazis, and he lay between life and death in a hospital in Teheran.

Not much there to dispute the view about the good old days contrasted with how bad it was later. But that's the exception.

Let's look at some reasons to be grateful rather than gloomy about the present, especially concerning everyday things that we tend not to even notice any more because they are so familiar.

Firstly, and most importantly, you are alive. As a statement of the obvious this surely takes the gold medal. And yet…

Consider the alternative. Not seeing another sunrise. Never to experience again being with those you love most. Never to know what developments in cancer research may arise. Never to have any experiences ever again. Now for some people in very extreme circumstances, either real e.g. in a torture cell, or purely from a series of mental preludes they may indeed prefer death to remaining alive. But for most of us life is precious – if only we stop to think about it. Mindfulness trains you to notice the reality of the wonder and pricelessness of your moment by moment awareness of being alive.

Next, consider what actually keeps us alive practically. These are, in order of importance and urgency, the air we breathe, the water we drink, the food we eat, and the clothing and home that keep us warm and secure from the weather and the uncertainties of the outside world.

Despite our increased industrialising globally the air we breathe is cleaner than it has been for decades, this because of the brilliance of our scientists and technologists, and the adoption of regulations and new methods, albeit very slowly, by our political leaders. The air we breathe is still not harmless but it has reduced in toxicity and is still improving. This means our children are likely to breathe even purer air than us.

We get our drinking water mostly from a tap. It is paid for by taxation so is free at point of need i.e. whenever we are thirsty. It is pure enough not to give us diseases or illness, and it is utterly essential for our continued existence. People less than ten hours flight from Scotland die from drinking unclean water virtually every day. Some die from a lack of any water at all. Yet we have it beautifully cool and clean via the rain that falls so magnificently from the clouds over our heads, into reservoirs created to keep us alive and healthy. From there the water goes via water purifications plants to mile upon mile of pipes until it emerges sparkling into our glass from the tap.

This in my opinion is akin to a miracle. Mindfulness practice is to just notice the reality of this. The beauty of good thinking, long-term investment, and a compassionate collective mindset. 3000 people died in Glasgow of cholera, a water-borne disease, in 1832. We live without that fear, without that tragedy. Notice this with a clear, gentle awareness when you next fill your glass with water, and be grateful that we have this.

There are a thousand other things we can be grateful for, from mobile phones and social media, to global travel for most in the rich world and so much else.

None of this is to forget or ignore the plight of others. But for you to be mentally well and physically energised enough to fully live your life you need nourished by thoughts and awareness of all reality, not just the bad stuff. The scientific evidence is unequivocal: think pessimistically and you die younger. You also get tired more easily and more regularly, a condition hardly conducive to enjoying life or helping greater causes.

There is so much to be done still. Innocent die of hunger (and thirst). We have the disgrace of a need for food banks, of increased homelessness. All utterly unacceptable.

But in the midst of our compassion and concern for others remember that there is much to be grateful for, so notice it. Be mindful and allow gratitude to build deep inside you.

Let it All Go

How much do you think about? You could probably name about four or five things off the top of your head but I bet if you actually watched your mind closely day in day out for a few days you'd realise you think about hundreds of different things. Some things you probably think about dozens of times a week. The weather. Have I remembered my purse or wallet? I'll just lock the back door. Does the car need petrol? These are the relatively trivial things.

Much more serious things pervade our mind. Hope the kids are OK. Another terror attack could happen anywhere. What if so and so gets elected next week? I can't take much more of the stress that my work makes me feel.

Moreover, we tend not to deliberately think about these things. They just appear in our head, as if by chance. However it's not by chance. As we know everything happens because of some previous event. It's like the weather forecast. Forecasters can predict with reasonable accuracy what the weather will be like tomorrow because they see the patterns from previous days.

It's the same with the thoughts, feelings and emotions that arise in our head. If we could know the billions of past experiences you've had, plus the influences of your genes, then theoretically we could predict your response to some future event.

That's actually quite scary isn't it? As if we're more like a computer programme, pre-set to act in predictable ways than a truly free-thinking, unconditioned living example of human intelligence. It's a bit like Keanu Reaves as the character Neo in The Matrix, a science fiction film in which humans only think they're living a life but are in fact actually being used as batteries for sentient machines which have taken over the world.

It's not quite as bad as that but living our life being affected in predictable ways by external experiences or events, internal genetic impulses, or conditioned ways of thinking is hardly a great vision of living a full, free and vibrant life.

So what can we do about this? The scientific research shows us quite clearly. We can use the natural skill we call mindfulness. This allows us to notice the automatic responses as they happen. That's stage one, what Sri Lankan Buddhists call Bare Awareness. So it's just noticing. Not judging. Not yet trying to change anything.

What we're doing when practicing in this way is building up the strength of this skill we have. It's literally just practice. The more we do it the better we get at it.

So over time we get better at being mindful, Our Bare Awareness strengthens and sharpens.

That's stage one. Now instead of simply unconsciously reacting to something with irritation, we now see that irritation has arisen.

This then sets us up for the second stage. Deciding what to do about our automatic reaction.

You can't change your mind unless you're aware of what your mind is doing at any moment. Once you are aware you can use the wiser, more reflective and rational aspects of our mind to assess the likely outcome or outcomes of what's currently happening automatically in our head. In this case it is irritation.

We reason that irritation is likely to cause us no good, and possibly some negative results. Moreover if we have used some of our time to study and learn about how the mind and body are affected by emotions and thoughts, we will remember that irritation in our mind speeds up the body's aging process and makes us a bit more likely to catch the next series of bugs that come along. Moreover being irritated makes us more likely to be irritable in future. In other words it strengthens that particular habitual response in us.

So, seeing all these likely outcomes from our automatic irritation enables us to decide that we don't want this irritation to fully blossom inside us or be expressed to the outside world.

What then are our options?

In the early stages of mindfulness we can switch the attention gently and subtly to our breath, or something similarly neutral and pleasant like noticing the softness of our tee shirt on our skin.

For reasons we don't know yet, this has a different, more positive effect than forcibly suppressing our negative emotion. Simply notice the breath lightly but clearly, especially at the tip of the nostrils, or at the diaphragm, or alternatively at the lungs as they fill and empty.

This allows our negative feeling to diminish, often vanish. Job done.

A more advanced version of this is to deliberately use the negative feeling as a form of learning. In this situation instead of noticing the breath in order to take the mind's attention away from the irritation it currently possesses, we instead try to gently but clearly notice the emotion of irritability itself.

This is harder as it runs the risk of switching the mind back to the very thing that you want to fade away. However the benefit from doing this effectively is great. We get to see the monstrous and petty nature of some of our raw emotions and reactions. The more familiar we become, the better able to let them go.

We may never quite gain total liberation from our mind's conditioning, but we can increasingly remove ourselves from the worst of our Matrix-like autopilot way of living.

Mindful Walking

More and more people are walking nowadays. I see it locally when I'm out and about, at Hamilton's extensive Palace Grounds, at Strathclyde Park where people walk around the loch, and at Chatelherault Country Park. It's great to see people outside.

People walk for many reasons. Let's exclude the obvious one of getting from A to B for the moment. People walk for their health. Power walkers, upright and fast moving, arms swinging, treat walking as an alternative to running, cycling or swimming for cardio-vascular or aerobic exercise.

Others walk at a moderate pace, often with a friend. This tends to be a combination of companionship, enjoying being outdoors, and a modest degree of fitness activity.

Many people walk their dog, which in turn becomes the dog giving them a walk, for the usual combination of reasons, health and fitness and sheer enjoyment. The added factor of the loyalty and fun of a dog as a pet is clear when you see how people interact with their pets on these walks.

A smaller number of people walk primarily to clear their mind or to help them manage something problematic or painful in their life.

These people tend to walk more slowly than others, as if the slow pace of the steps allows their mind to ponder their predicaments and enable solutions to arise. This works, and it's what great scientists, from Einstein, Newton and Darwin did almost as daily practices.

Then there's something called mindful walking.

When we walk mindfully we don't do it to become fitter, though that may be a side-effect. We don't do it for companionship, even if others are with us. Nor do we do it to free up our mind or to ruminate or ponder something that's bothering us.

We do it as part of our wider mindfulness practice, whose aim is to free our minds of all the conditioned junk, harmful states, and unhelpful habits we've picked up from our genes and our life experiences. But we don't think about these aims when we walk mindfully because that's rumination and pondering. If you want to think about something while walking that's fine but don't mistake it for mindful walking. They are two entirely different things, producing entirely different results.

When we walk mindfully we walk slowly. We walk slowly so we're better able to notice things. Logically it's harder to notice things if we're moving fast. Mindfulness is after all, paying attention on purpose to what's going on moment by moment.

How do we notice when walking mindfully? Use your five senses. I tend to just allow my mind to move from sense to sense, because my mind is now used to doing these practices. This means my mind tends to linger for some time on one thing, then it moves onto another. We just notice for the sake of noticing. Not to enjoy what we notice, nor to take a note of it, nor to think about it. It's raw, bare awareness. Noticing for its own sake.

If you're starting this practice there's a danger in just allowing your mind to wander in the way I've just described. A mind which is not yet trained in mindfulness will readily and quickly wander to worries, plans, concerns, daydreams, and it may be several minutes before you realise that you are no longer being mindful of what's going on in the here and now. So for that reason you might want to start a bit more methodically. Give say roughly twenty or thirty seconds to each of the four main senses we have available to us when walking, assuming you're not eating on the walk, so the fifth sense, taste, is not activated. So, just notice what you see for a short period. Say it's a bird feeding on the football park. Just notice it, what it does, how it moves. Don't makes any judgements about it, though it's fine for you to notice any immediate pleasure or dislike arising in your mind as you see it.

After twenty or thirty seconds deliberately change your attention to what you hear. It could be the traffic, or bird songs, perhaps the rustle of leaves in a tree as the wind blows through them. Again, just notice gently, lightly, without making inner comments about what you perceive through your ears.

Then on to the sense of touch. What do your steps feel like, as the heel then the balls of the feet complete a step? How does your ankle work when you step? What does it feel like physically? And your knee? Hip joint? Arms? Shoulders? Just feel it all without trying to think about it or judge it in any way.

Still on the sense of touch, you can notice the feeling of the air or wind on your cheeks, your hair, your hands and fingers. You can even notice the soft feeling of your clothing on your skin, especially at the shoulders and top of the arms.

Finally, occasionally you can notice smells. Pleasant, unpleasant, it doesn't matter.

Then repeat the cycle of the four senses for as long as you want to do it.
This is particularly effective for people with anxiety and serious worries as it allows the mind to gently focus on everyday things, and is a useful alternative for people who feel they can't focus properly doing classic mindfulness practices with their eyes closed in a room in completer silence.

So go out, give it a try, and just enjoy the beauty of noticing.

A Little Self-Restraint

W.B. Yeats put it beautifully

"The best lack all conviction, while the worst
Are full of passionate intensity"

In the lead up to the General Election I witnessed more unpleasant, unnecessary and deliberately provocative messages on social media than I have seen for a long time. At one level it's completely understandable. A huge amount was at stake at a Scottish, a UK, and of course, a European level. Some people feel passionately about certain issues, and have a fervent belief in the rightness of their opinion and the moral or logical righteousness of their cause.

But a question or two does arise in my head for these people. In the classic words of Crocodile Dundee, Don't they have mates? Or more importantly, don't they have family to be with, or places they can go out and walk around?

Yet I find myself doing it too. At a spare moment we just check to see if something new has come up on Facebook or Twitter, then get caught up by our negative reaction to someone's post. The annoyance or a desire to retort stirs up in our mind and we type it up and hit the send or post button.

Job done. Or so we think. But for every retort we write there is likely to be at least one reply coming our way.

The reply is likely to dispute our view, which probably annoys us again, and the temptation arises to respond in kind yet again.

Moreover, other similar comments start to grab our attention.

Meanwhile time slips by, our mood tightens up and feels negative, and there is no final victory in the tit for tat messaging unless our side finally wins, giving us the opportunity to finally stick it to our online rivals, mocking them for the defeat they have just suffered.

All of which is of course within our rights to do. My point however is about wellbeing, a happy, fulfilled life, and choosing what to do in each moment. The internet is full of good things, fun things, harmless things, but it is also full of evidence of people unthinkingly knee-jerk reacting and thus being blown this way and that by whatever content they come across. The result; wasted time, tiredness, and a sense of emptiness because the activity had been so bereft of anything that actually matters in your life.

Mindfulness asks us to become so good at noticing what's actually going on in our life, that we are finally able to discern between the rubbish around us and that which nurtures our very being. The more rubbish we intake or participate in, the less developed we become as a person. Our energy wanes. Our enthusiasm drops. Our sense of love and joy for others and for life itself ebbs away.

We not only forget that we have blinkers on, we tighten them further and further, making us more and more narrow-minded and conditioned with every passing day.

Part of restoring a sense of freshness and mental energy to your life is to put into place some degree of self-restraint. Instant self-gratification and knee-jerk reaction do satisfy, but only for a very short time, whilst dealing with the consequences of our self-indulgence can last a lifetime.

Practise trying to notice. It's very easy to do so every so often, when the mind remembers, but it takes a lot of time and effort to cultivate that way of being, so that your mind is able to notice more and more moments in the day. The more moments you notice the more you start to be able to catch yourself in those moments when our mind has gone completely off-track, wasting precious time on trash, or worse, causing hurt to ourselves through slipshod, mindless actions and reactions.

Here's an extreme example. The average person in the UK now spends around four hours per day watching television.

Being conservative, if you stopped watching television altogether and studied instead you could get a university degree every six years. So if you are forty years old, you could achieve a doctorate, change career, read all the world's top thousand classic books, and still spend more time with your family and friends if you live the average lifespan.

Add in the time we spend on Facebook, Twitter and so on, and there's almost nothing we couldn't do with the time we'd save. So rather than arguing with the political opposition online, or present the Like button on messages that we agree with, we could actually stop and think how we might help create a better society or improve the lives of people, animals, or the environment, whether your focus is local or global.

It's about that time in an article when the liberal in me thinks I'd have to add "of course we don't have to give up all of our down time or the little things we enjoy" but actually when you look at it the way I've just explained it, the opposite is true. We should Actually give up all the time-wasting activities we do. The gift of life deserves better treatment. The astonishing reality of being alive, able to sense with five senses, reason with the brain, and feel myriad emotions and passions and enthusiasm, demands that we are mindful enough to make the most of the miracle of our own existence.

Dealing With Negativity Bias

Today, in 1950, North Korea invaded South Korea starting what we call the Korean War. Some sixty-seven years on the two countries remain divided and tensions are higher that they have been for several years. Many people's automatic reaction is that we, as a species, are condemned to repeat the past. Even the great English historian A. J. P. Taylor once said that history was "just one damned thing after another".

However Taylor was also wise enough on another occasion to say "Nothing is inevitable until it happens".

These are examples of the mind's tendency to try to see order in life, especially with regards to suffering. The great ancient religions and philosophies of India called it karma, the idea that there is a natural law which dictates that our intentions or actions result in ways that will either haunt or reward us at some point in the future.

I'm not a believer in karma but it's a basic law of physics that every action will cause reactions of one sort or another. We also know that our emotions or human activities often result in ripples that affect the people around us. At a neuroscience level, the concept of neuroplasticity dictates that our mind is constantly being shaped, moulded and remoulded by our every experience, which in effect is just another example of cause and effect, karma of sorts.

There are two issues concerning these points that I'd like to explore. The first is some people's tendency over time to see things in a pessimistic light or indeed to get irritated more easily. Think of the "grumpy old man" stereotype. The other is the potential for us to gain an increasing degree of control over how our minds are shaped by external events and our reactions to these.

I have a sense that negative experiences weigh more heavily than positive ones. I can't see much research on this matter, maybe because it is difficult to measure the impact of one event against another. But there are some obvious major life examples which can make the point. Consider a wedding, or the birth of a daughter or son. These are for many people "the happiest day of my life". Then consider something awful. Being diagnosed with cancer, or loving someone you love dearly. Feel how they weigh on your mind, or in your heart. A wedding or a birth may be special but the excitement and joy tend to lose their shine with the everyday realities of marriage or bringing up kids. We may still love our spouse or children dearly, and look back on our wedding and the birth with nostalgic pleasure but over time these events don't remain on our minds as a day to day presence.

However the sense of having had cancer, and the potential for it to recur, or the lifelong sadness many of us feel embedded within regarding the loss of those we love, do continue to weigh on our minds, and often affect the tone of our life frequently from day to day. So I believe negative emotions are, if you like, heavier in feel and effect than positive ones, and they hang around for a much longer time.

Over the years and decades therefore we can become increasingly filled with the effect of these negative experiences whereas the lighter happy ones seem to arise then dwindle from our minds. Result, an increasingly negative version of who we are dominates.

Which brings me to my second point. We can deliberately use the brain's neuroplastic quality to help ensure that we don't suffer from this tendency to become more negative or pessimistic in the world as we get older. Because our mind tends to consolidate and strengthen our negative views and habits over time we must therefore deliberately and continuously combat that tendency.

There are many simple and common sense ways of doing this. As is explained every week by my fellow column writers in the Sunday Herald Magazine, fitness and exercise, eating healthily, and simply getting outdoors more often, have a positive effect not only on our body but on our state of mind. So take their advice seriously and do what you know is good for you, while reducing what is not.

Mindfulness is however, the most direct and powerful way we can combat our tendency to see life through a dark lens. The brilliant research by neuroscientists, psychologists and doctors over the past thirty years have shown that mindfulness practices as simple as noticing what it is actually like to feel and taste a piece of fruit, fully, slowly and in a savouring way, does combat those negative mental tendencies.

Regular and ongoing paying attention to any experience of the five senses, or indeed of the mind and its content itself can reverse much of the mental junk we have accumulated over time. Moreover it can and does replace it with an absolutely beautiful combination of fine mental qualities. Clarity of thought.

Calmness even when a crisis or argument occurs. Contentment and love of being alive. Compassion and consideration for others, and not just humans, but animals, the environment, everything that is part of the natural world.

It is hard to overstate how good these qualities are in making your life more meaningful and more enjoyable. It does not deny, nor ignore the horrors of life, human and natural, but it does free us from the delusion that everything is worse than it used to be, and instead remind us that so very much is miles better than what we had in the past.

Your Life as a Work of Art

In the past thirty years neuroscientists have coined the term neuroplasticity. Neuro means the nerves, the parts of the body that act as a network for the brain, sending and receiving messages, almost like a railway network. Plastic originally meant, and in fields of science still means, the ability to be shaped, moulded, or reshaped. So neuroplasticity means the property of our own mind to be changed over time. In actual fact it is changed every moment of your life, by your every experience, whether that's something mundane and unnoticed, or something seismic in your life.

The aim must be to increase the degree of control over these changes. We are already pre-programmed by our genes to react in certain ways under specific circumstances. The three most primal of these are our responses to hunger and thirst, our fight or flight reaction when we sense danger, and our sexual drive, nature's way of ensuring we sustain the gene pool.

These are all about survival but life is much more than that, and other ways we have been shaped by our genes and life experiences are much less helpful or meaningful. Things like irritation, impatience, getting things way out of proportion, family rows over nothing. These are all ways we have been shaped and changed by life, much to our disadvantage when it comes to trying to enjoy a rich, fulfilled and happy life.

But if we are neuroplastic then that can be seen too in a positive light. Rather than bemoan the habits that we have accrued through this process, we can think of ourselves as something we can deliberately shape, in our own time to our own requirements. Imagine your life as a work of art, or rather a canvas. There's already a full painting on the canvas, but with a bit of effort we can scrape off that bit we don't like in the top left, change the mood or colour, which in turn changes the overall painting a bit.

This is how many of the great artists did their work. Art restorers often find when doing their incredibly detailed and careful work, that underneath a famous painting are earlier details which the artist decided not to keep. In some extreme cases a painting has been made over an earlier completed work. Pablo Picasso worked at lightning speed, creating tens of thousands of painting and sculptures. If he didn't like the way something was going, he would just pain over it, or in the case of a sculpture, break a bit off, or bend a piece of metal into a different shape.

Mindfulness helps us bend the bits of metal that make up who we are, helps us scrape off the paint that we feel in retrospect are not helpful in the work of art that is our life.

You don't even need to have an idea of what the finished version of you would look like. Just be gently noticing moment by moment you start to see aspects of who you are that you'd like to just let go of; in time, with practice noticing, these old encrusted habits will start to flake off.

You will also start to see traits which are already instilled in you, that you feel are healthy and nurturing. Through mindfully noticing these you can build their strength, developing the potential of these feelings to arise more powerfully and regularly through time.

Three of our finest traits, clarity of thought, calmness, and a sense of altruistic compassion for others, can be deliberately nurtured simply by paying attention to the flow of air in and out of our lungs as we breathe. Harvard and Oxford amongst other universities have shown this to be the case. Just a few minutes of quiet, meditative attention on our breathing can help you reformat who you are.

This takes time. It's a long-term game. Your life is your masterpiece, the only work of art you really have to create. It's always a work in progress, so don't worry about flaws or imperfections. Just use mindfulness so that you, and not outside circumstances, are the artist dictating what you create.

Knee-jerk Reactions

Your mind's reaction to situations is like Spotify or your downloaded music, or for those of us old enough to remember, like a juke box. In those examples simply press a certain button and a song will start. If you press for a particular Adele song you won't get Eminem. The technology is not programmed to do that. The reaction to you pressing a certain tab is predictable.

When your mind is not responding to anything in particular it's, like Spotify or the juke box set to random play. Anything might pop up into your mind from the vast stores of thoughts, ideas, emotions, memories, moods, desires, or dislikes that have collated day after day through your entire life to date. Logically we know that there must be a mechanism inside the brain or body that triggers these seemingly random thoughts and feelings but as we don't know the science of it yet we think of it as completely chosen by chance.

So this is who we are. This is how we are. Programmed by past experiences and our genes to respond in particular ways to particular situations, and in between such events, to be the passive recipient of whatever things pop into our head.

It's not all bad. In fact some of it is great. An old song pops into our head that we haven't thought of for years, and we can sing along to it in our mind. We get a great idea for a celebration, or a gift, or even for a breakthrough in some important field like preventing or curing cancer.

Everything good that humanity has created, from poetry to beautiful gardens, from water purification plants that save the lives of billions to the new bridge across the Forth, has to have emerged as an idea from someone's mind before anything else could be done.

But some of it is bad, really bad. Just look at history. Just look at the troubles in so many different parts of the world today. They're the result of reactions, responses, ideas, desires, fears, hatreds, all of which originated in the mind of one or more persons. And while none of us is a Hitler, none of us is an angel either. Our minds contain, deep in its huge storage of possible reactions, both the gracious and the destructive.

So we need to be able to deal with the unhealthy, the unhelpful, or the downright awful reactions our mind impels us to put into action.

And to be able to deal with such reactions we need to notice them clearly as they arise. These creations of the mind arise lightning fast so unless we are equally quick to notice them they will sweep you away into their path before you know it. This then usually causes a whole chain of causes and effects, leaving us and others in a bad place before we know it.

Which is where the practice of mindfulness comes in. Mindfulness is a natural tool or skill of the mind, but it tends to be quite weak in comparison with the dominant automatic response mechanism of the mind. The mind prefers to be automatic. It's easier, habitual, effortless. So we need to deliberately cultivate our ability to be mindful.

You can do it right now while reading this article. Notice the sensation of your legs and back on the chair you're sitting in, or your feet touching the ground if you're standing. Try and allow your attention to become light and relaxed, the opposite of heavy focussed concentration. Notice any parts of your body that are hard pressed into the chair or floor. Just note how it feels to your body or mind, but don't judge it, don't react to it. Now notice any parts that, while in contact with the chair or the floor, are much less so than the first parts. Be aware of just how softly the body can be in touch with an object and still feel it clearly. Then gently and slowly let this awareness leave the chair or floor, and allow your clear focus to return solely to the newspaper.

That's it. Simple isn't it? Yet this is what, over time, will help you become in control of those knee-jerk or unwanted reactions that your mind will produce. Try it. You'll be amazed.

Tapping Into Something Deeper

We've all had those moments. You're sitting listening to a song or looking at a view and it hits you. You get a shiver up your spine or your eyes start to well up. Something in the music, the lyrics, or what you've just seen, has pierced through our normal shallow receptors and gone somewhere way deeper and more primal. These are precious and potentially hugely insightful moments of raw experience.

There's a piece of modern classical music by a recently deceased Polish composer, Henrik Gorecki. From his Symphony No. 3 (Symphony of Sorrowful Songs), the second piece is unbearably poignant to me, yet still beautiful and nurturing of all that is good in people. It's a very understated, minimalist piece but it rends the heart. The short lyrics are directly from words carved into the wall of a Gestapo cell in Krakow, Poland. Written there by an eighteen year old girl, it reads

Mama, no, don't weep.
Most pure Queen of Heaven
Protect me always
Ave Maria

Even writing about it makes me well up. To experience the full impact of this astonishing work it's best to go onto You Tube and Search for Gorecki Isabel (that's the soloist's first name) and it'll be the first link that appears.

The film is a work of art in its own right, complementing the music and lyrics impeccably. It is set in Auschwitz with the orchestra playing in the camp itself. The soloist, Isabel Bayrakdaraian, sings at the doorway looking out into the dark as snow falls onto the concrete. Read the comments and you get a sense of what this short piece of music does to the human heart.

Not much hits me as powerfully as this, but many other things do make a deep impact. The scene in To Kill A Mockingbird – the book, or the film – where the hero, Scout, a young girl, recognises Boo Radley near the end of the book. You have to know the back story to get why this works so powerfully, and if you don't know it, go buy both the book and the film, they are gems. Scout says "Hi Boo" then a few minutes later she takes his hand and leads him out of the room. It is a moment of great beauty and sensitivity.

My final example is not something I experienced but which I witnessed my wife experience way back before we got married. I had been working and travelling my way around the world for the best part of four years in the 1980s and she came to see me for a short time in Mexico in the Easter of 1986. I took her to see the Diego Rivera fresco masterpiece "Man at the Crossroads".

It depicts a man in the centre, dressed in scientific protective type clothing and gloves, with something resembling four giant electrons pulses emanating around him, and a big metallic cylindrical machine above his head.

Beyond that the world is in turmoil. Created in 1934 it shows the political tensions of the time. Fascists to his right, communist marchers to the left. Lenin, Darwin, Marx and the mass of mankind are all represented, whilst below is the world of plants and nature.

I love his work so was thrilled to see it. My wife Christine came along because I wanted to see it but she was the one who was deeply affected by it. It's his face, his eyes, she said. She was right. His face looks fraught, stress, anxious, worn out; the immensity and complexity of the world around him seemingly impossible to control.

Rivera's depiction went straight through all the usual inner defensive mechanisms we have and struck Christine deep in her heart.

This is mindfulness happening naturally through great art. With practice we can enable such feelings to happen on a daily, even frequent basis, with each experience softly but surely building up our empathy, compassion and love of life. Instead of having to wait for a moment of great artistry or genius, we can experience it watching a field of hay, or a patch of blue sky on a cloudy day.

The Independence of the Individual

The great Scottish journalist Neal Ascherson wrote a typically thought-provoking piece earlier this month in the Sunday Herald in which he argued – and made as his essay's title – Why Scotland must act as an independent nation. It garnered the usual plethora of comments in response, from both sides of the indy argument, more measured than usual, perhaps because of the esteem with which the author is held, and the subtle way he framed his argument, more philosophical and less didactic than most writings on this vexed subject.

I don't wish to be drawn into that particular argument as there are more than enough able contributors, while too few focus on my main area of interest, the wellbeing of people regardless of how they vote on any issue. However Neal's commentary reminded me in tone and stance of the great American philosopher and activist Henry David Thoreau. Rather than say Scotland should act as if it was independent, Thoreau argued that each of us should act as if we were what Thoreau proclaimed we already are, sovereign in our own right.

Thoreau went to jail for not paying his Taxes in 1846 because he refused to support a U.S. government which would not abolish slavery and which had deliberately created an incident allowing the U.S. army to march into Mexico and eventually seize an enormous part of Mexico's territory (around 15% of the present day America.)

However it was not Thoreau's going to jail that mattered to him – ironically a friend paid his taxes for him the following day so he was released after one day. What concerned him was the principle. Always follow your conscience, and when, as sometimes must happen, your values and those of the State clash, you should not meekly accept the authority of the State, but oppose it in whatever way you can.

This is the opposite of what we currently accept as democracy, which is in effect, the tyranny of the majority, at best, more often the tyranny of whoever won the most seats. But again I want to state I am not looking at this from a political perspective so bear with me.

From this experience Thoreau grew more and more involved in supporting the anti-slavery movement. In 1848 he delivered a series of lectures, one of which when printed became known as Civil Disobedience. It was to have an enormous impact on history, with Tolstoy, Gandhi and Martin Luther King all directly citing his influence on their thinking and strategies.

In the essay version Thoreau says we are personally disgraced by immoral actions of our government, even if we never voted for them or didn't support the particular policies with which we morally disagree.

What does this have to do with mindfulness? Everything. We do not live in a vacuum. We are part of our local community, which is part of wider society.

Regardless of political persuasion the government which runs our affairs, at local, Scottish, British and for the next year or more, European, do so in the name of us all.

Mindfulness has a three-fold stage of thinking. The first is to notice in each moment what is actually going on. The second is to do so with a particular alertness for thoughts or actions that may be unhealthy or unacceptable. The third is to think clearly and calmly in order to make the most of each moment. Where a moment recognises injustice, unfairness, unpleasantness, harm or suffering whether self-created or caused by someone or something outside of yourself, we should act in order to minimise the hurt or harm, and in its place create what you consider will result in a better outcome.

So using as a template Neal's urging that Scotland should act as if it is already independent, I would say that, with clarity, calmness and compassion, we should all act as if we, as individuals, family members, work colleagues, friends, neighbours, and yes, citizens, were sovereign, and we should try to find ways of expressing our fundamental disagreement with any action, whether by people or institutions, workplaces or governments, when such disagreements occur.

We need to act in accordance with this reality, that each of us is already independent.

Who do you think you are?

We live with a strong image of ourselves in our mind. We can picture our face, what it looks like, and we have an idea of what our personality is. According to researchers however we usually see as our true self the best version of how we behave, what we think, how we communicate. Those times when we're tetchy, irritated, worry, prejudiced… they're all just off-moments. In short we idealise ourselves.

Yet what a whole plethora of research has found is that we are much less of a fixed, positive personality than we think, in two ways. Firstly we're not that rock solid at all. A brilliant study by Harvard University showed that our minds wander to daydreams, concerns, past regrets, bitterness, and fantasies almost half of our waking moments. So far from being "me" we are more like the tickertape of headlines that runs along the bottom of the news channels, except than in our case there's no main story running at the same time. Who we are IS the tickertape of distractions.

Secondly, given that our mind wanders so frequently, and we know that get irritated and annoyed in minor ways several times a day, the version that we imagine to be our true self, the one where all our negative mental habits are airbrushed out of the picture, is fake. What we actually are, is a flickering, ever-shifting set of responses that exist anywhere on a spectrum that runs from saintly to horrifically self-centred or hateful. Imagine that on your passport under the heading: Defining Characteristics.

Moreover most of us consider ourselves to be of a national identity. I think I'm Scottish. Granted my dad was Polish. Oh, and all of my mother's antecedents were Irish through and through going back to the famines of the 1840s when Daniel Murphy came over to Scotland with his young wife and family. So although born in Cambuslang, speaking with a Lanarkshire accent, there's not a drop of Scottish blood in me.

Does that matter? Not now, not according to mainstream thought anyway. If you're here you're Scottish, say the Scottish Government and all the main political parties. But what does it mean anyway, to say I'm Scottish? And if you the reader consider yourself Scottish, can you say in what way? To what extent? I have no ethnic Scottishness in me, but then the people called Scots came from Ireland in the first place, so if I go back far enough do I become de facto Scottish?

Note that this has nothing to do with politics, the independence referendum, the Union, even Brexit. And yet, it does. How we see ourselves, in terms of national identity, and how we see "others" in terms of their national identity, and how we perceive the relationship between "us" and those "others" all affect how we think "our" country should be defined and governed. See how complex it becomes? I've had to put so many quotation marks over those words "us" and "others" because each of us might have a different definition of who we mean by those terms.

It's all fake.

There is no us and them except in our minds. There is no land – real land, the solid bit of the surface of the Earth – called Scotland, or the United Kingdom, or the European union or even Europe. There are seven or eight major solid parts of the Earth's crust, called tectonic plates, with many more minor ones. The one Scotland is on is not only part of the same bit of what we'd call land as the rest of the UK, but also all of Europe, much of Asia, and half of the land under the Atlantic Ocean. It's called the Eurasian Plate. How we split it up into continents, countries, regions, and so on is just history, or what A.J.P. Taylor called "one damned thing after another".

Mindfulness is all about noticing. In this instance we can learn to notice our preconceived ideas of ourselves, our different identities including our national ones, and how these things condition our thinking politically one way or another. It's absolutely fine to have different political aims and to have a view of ourselves as who we are, but it is hugely helpful in our lives if we can see the degree to which we've been programmed and to rid ourselves of those programmes and try to see the complexity of life in a clearer less blinkered way. Mindfulness will help you do this.

Let It Go

Today is Hiroshima Day, one of the most notorious days in human history. On this day in 1945 70,000 people in the Japanese city were killed by a single atomic bomb, with tens of thousands dying of radiation sicknesses in the days, weeks, months and years that followed. It was the first of only two nuclear weapons ever used in human history, the other being three days later on the Japanese city of Nagasaki.

I have had the privilege of visiting Hiroshima, its Peace Memorial Park, and its Peace Memorial Museum. The one thing that struck me, aside from all the sites, photographs, and emotions we'd all expect from such a tragic city, was how beautiful, spacious and peaceful it is for such a large city (its population is over one million).

If you go onto Google and search for Hiroshima under Images, almost all you get is endless black and white images of the nuclear explosion or the devastating effect it had on the city or the victims. However if you search for "Hiroshima now" you find an entirely different city. It has only recovered, it has been reborn.

One of the things that mindfulness has helped me enormously with in my life is this understanding that things move on, but that often we do not move on with them. We get mentally stuck in images and views of past events, and this deeply affects how we see life. This can be how you perceive yourself, family members, your career, as well as political and social matters.

Consider just this short list plucked out of my head at random: not letting go of your partner's past error of judgement, not letting go of your own mistakes or poor decisions, bigotry or prejudice or other forms of narrow disapproval, Mrs. Thatcher, success or failure at school, arguments with your work colleagues or manager, traumatic events such as violence, major accidents, abuse, bullying, and the loss of someone we loved dearly.

Almost everyone carries at least one of these things around in their mind, which are events long since passed, or views formed decades ago. These weigh us down. We are so used to their presence in us, as part of who we are, that we usually don't even notice them. But they colour our every moment, or to describe it more accurately, they dilute the colour in our every moment, making it greyer, darker. The potential joy in the moment is extinguished by what negative baggage we unwittingly carry around.
Two great eastern teachers have commented on this natural tendency in people.

The Vietnamese monk Thich Nhat Hanh teaches us to ask ourselves the question "Am I sure?" when a negative thought, feeling or memory arises.

The Japanese Zen master Kosho Uchiyama put it more directly. "Open the hand of thought.". In other words, what pops us into our head from time to time is so useless, so unhelpful, even so poisonous that the best thing we can do about it is just to let it fall into non-existence.

This is pure mindfulness. Awareness of what's happening in the moment; noticing whether what's happening is nurturing, neutral, or negative; then deciding what to do depending on our assessment of what we notice.

The more we drop that is unhelpful, the lighter we become mentally. We feel freed up, liberated, A sense of zest and fun returns. Life is seen as something to play in. The moment is, as my old Tibetan Buddhist teacher Tharchin put it, "a field of potential".

To attain that mental state you need to dislodge and master all the junk and toxins that have become stuck in your head. This takes time, effort, and regular practice of mindfulness. Whether it's just noticing the way the clouds drift across the sky, rather than ruminating on an unpleasant meeting, or sitting formally noticing the way the breath enters and exists your body at the nostrils, it's the same practice.

Lao Tzu, credited with writing the Chinese classic Tao te Ching, wrote "the Sage is devoted to non-action". Letting go is non-action. Try it. If Hiroshima can let go, without forgetting the lessons of its terrible day seventy-two years ago today, then surely we all can.

A Mindful Take on Sentencing and Justice

The Scottish public are to be given a say on how offenders are sentenced in our courts. My gut reaction was one of horror, notwithstanding the democratic sentiment that such a consultation suggests. But, being mindful, I let go of my gut reaction and decided that this might be an interesting subject for the readers of the Sunday Herald.

So why my horror? It's a result of reading hundreds of abusive and aggressive comments on social media. If someone posts on Facebook or Twitter that a crime has been committed, a common response is the single expletive, SCUM! This comes as no surprise. The media is constantly full of stories of extreme language and threats on social media, especially to women.

I think that the view portrayed by William Golding in his classic novel Lord of the Flies is correct, namely that what we think of as civilisation, and take for granted, is paper thin, and if torn apart by circumstances, all hell could let loose. We witnessed this in the fall of Yugoslavia and the genocidal murders that followed.

When we see baying crowds shouting abuse and banging aggressively on prison vans which carry major offenders to prison, it is not difficult to imagine these becoming lynch mobs if not for the police.

From a mindfulness perspective we try not to judge such people, only to state the reality that some people's minds automatically react with great violence and desire for revenge and harm on people accused of serious crimes.

Ironically the lack of restraint that is dominant in some of us is, from a scientific perspective, virtually identical to the mindset of those who commit the crimes in a flash of anger or hatred.

Still looking at the subject from a scientific viewpoint, there is a major debate brewing in the legal profession, particularly in America. The point of contention is free-will. For millennia philosophers have debated whether we have free will. Do we really have control over our decisions and actions? This was a matter of huge importance in Christianity. After all it claims that God is all-knowing, therefore He knows in advance how we will live our lives. If that's the case how can anyone claim to say we have free will if it's all preordained.

That subject is far too big a subject for now but it does lead to important considerations for the government's consultation, especially as now we have objective scientific evidence that strongly suggests that our brain decides on a matter before we think we've made the decision. Let me put that another way, because it is pivotal to crime and punishment. While we think we're still internally debating whether to do this or that, our brain has in fact made the decision. We think we make rational choices; we actually have those decisions made for us by the unconscious automatic workings of the mind.

So to the subject at hand. If a man or woman in a particular situation commits a crime then are they really to blame? If the brain decides for us no matter how much we think we're considering the options are we really responsible for the brain's final decision?

It's too early to reach definitive conclusions on these findings but they can help us look at the consultation on sentencing in a new light. For eons the point of sentences in courts was twofold; to punish, that is to cause hurt or harm or pain to an offender; and to meet the demand for what we call "justice". But justice is in the eye of the beholder and often it is a high falutin euphemism for revenge.

What if we viewed people who commit crimes as victims of their own brains? We'd still need to protect the public from those brains if the evidence suggests the likelihood of future offences. But we'd no longer be looking to punish or inflict revenge. We'd make the whole purpose of sentencing about what are the best ways to help offenders nurture their mind and its moral compass to prevent future offences. Until this was attained offenders would be kept apart from the public.

So we'd let go of the punishment and justice mentality and replace it with mental development. That is a mindful approach to sentencing.

Be Where You Are

So our usual summer of sunny days and dreich days is coming to an end. I noticed some very pretty pink, then violet and white, petals had fallen off their flowers and landed on the little stones that line parts of our garden. The contrast was striking and, to my mind at any rate, very aesthetically pleasing. I looked at them and enjoyed the sensations that they created in my mind, and though it was early morning and I had a busy day ahead, I lingered. I focussed very lightly and in a relaxed way so as just to enjoy the moments for as long as the sensations remained, and became as clearly aware of how I felt as possible, without making any strained effort. In total I guess this lasted about forty seconds or so.

Had I been mindless I'd still have noticed the petals, probably thought "they look nice" then went on my busy way. I would have received maybe two or three seconds of very light, shallow moments of enjoyment. Instead I magnified the intensity of the pleasure I received by, say, thirty or forty-fold; and I made the experience last twenty times more than it otherwise would have.

This, here in Hamilton. I'm not long back from a holiday in Switzerland, where we saw some of the world's most awesome sites, including major glaciers, and the Matterhorn, from way up on high. So my experience of the petals was not in that league. But that's not the point.

The point is that I'm no longer in Switzerland. I'm in Hamilton. Here is where matters, wherever here is for you at any given moment.

What is available for you right here, right now? This is local. As local as it gets. You have five senses. What do you see right now? What sounds exist for you right now? Keep the attention relaxed, effortless, light as a feather. What are you in touch with, I mean physically? A chair, the floor, a pavement or path, the clothes on your back, on your shoulders, on your feet? What do they actually feel like right now? Are you eating while you read this? If so, what are the tastes, and how does this register in your mind? Hopefully, as enjoyable, a pleasure. And is there any smell around? Be aware in your moment. Don't let the opportunities to fully experience life wash past you as if you were a senseless being, doomed only ever to be aware of endless thoughts and reflections and moods that your mind commands you to succumb to.

You can do this mindfulness anywhere. That's the whole point. The magnificent Buddhist teacher Thich Nhat Hanh, who has led the growing interest in mindfulness in the West since his arrival in exile from his native Vietnam, once told an audience, "Be free where you are.". Sounds like one of those trite positive lifestyle posters you see on Facebook every day. But he said it to an audience of more than one hundred and twenty inmates of a prison, the Maryland Correctional Institution in Haggerston.

He had to pass through sixteen checkpoints just to get to the hall. Imagine the situation. This is 1999, and a small, born-robed old Vietnamese man, sits in front of these restless prisoners and tells them they are free if they want to be.

By the time he finished his talk and mindfulness meditation many of the prisoners got it. They may be locked up in a jail, often in a small cell, but their quality of mind, their state of mind, the thoughts and feelings that they allowed to come fully into being, they could have the power to be in charge of these. They could be free where they are.

How about you then, in your relative comfort, relative places of beauty? Can you be free where you are right here where you are? Right now in the blink of a moment? I have found joy walking on the pavement along Mill Road, Hamilton. The joy came from my mind appreciating having a pavement, living in a community and society where pavements exist, and my appreciation of being able to walk, and yes, my appreciation of being free.

Summer's Almost Gone

In the words of the old Doors song "Summer's almost gone." How cheery a sentence for right now as August comes to an end and September prefers to blow with its mix of blustery winds and mixed weather, and the temperatures in general start to cool. At least we're not as gloomy as Jim Morrison, the singer of The Doors ends the song "The winter's coming on, summer's almost gone".

Yet isn't this what we do so often? We're not even at the end of something enjoyable and we look ahead to something less positive or fun taking its place. Many teachers, who have recently gone back to work for the new school year, have a growing sense of unease as July ends and August begins. People diagnosed with serious illnesses often can't help but agree with what Robert Burns writes at the end of To a Mouse "An' forward, tho' I canna see, I guess an fear!"

Meanwhile summer's just almost gone. It's not gone yet. Even when there are only minutes of sunshine left, literally or metaphorically, we can soak in the richness that those moments give us. Our worries, our concerns, and our pessimistic projections only serve to lay waste to the moments we have right here right now.

So what's going on in my life right now as I write this. I am in a nice wee room at home where I do my work when I'm not out and about delivering talks or mindfulness sessions, or having business meetings with family businesses and others from a variety of walk of life.

The room's temperature is moderate, pleasant. My chair is just the right combination of soft yet sturdy to make my body feel comfortable on it. I'm wearing an old long-sleeved tee shirt and a pair of baggy tracksuit bottoms, and a pair of soft socks on my feet. They all add to the physically felt sensation of comfort and softness around my body, which makes me mentally feel relaxed but free to think and create in a flowing manner.

Outside my front garden the sun shines, and our tiny wee almost triangular patch of grass is beautiful bright, like the stereotype we give to the island of Ireland when we think of emerald green. It is a delight to my mind, via my eyes. In contrast the two types of pebble stones that surround the grass are quite placid and low key in comparison, which highlights the grass's sharpness yet gives the whole garden a solid, firm look.

There are three kinds of long grasses in my range of vision too, all within the small front garden. They are of different shades of wheat colour, some almost bleached blond, others a little bit orange-tinged.
They're all blowing fairly strongly in the breeze, bringing life and movement to the scene. In front of each of two of the types of long grass lie a solid grey stone, like rocky islands on a dry stane loch. And that's what it's kind of meant to represent, very zen, fairly minimal. It's pleasing to my eye right now.

So I take a few seconds out from writing to enjoy it. A few seconds becomes thirty seconds. Just soaking in visual experiences that my brain registers as pleasant. I try not to judge it, analyse it, probe it.

Just purely and lightly experience it for all it's worth.

I notice the shadows. Over the near twenty years during which I have practiced and development my own mindfulness I have come to find shadows very aesthetically pleasing. I know for some people that will sound like a pretentious statement, but it just is what it is. I see shadows and really like them. Their shape. Their imprint if you like on the grass right now. On the pebbles. Shadows of trees, branches, of the grasses themselves, and as these latter objects blow, of course the shadows flow to and fro on the pebbles. And it is all just a joy.

Summer's almost gone. The daylight has not too long to go either. It's after 5pm as I write this. I have a choice. I can choose to think of the coming colder weather, or the darkness which will envelope my garden within the next three or four hours. I choose to absorb the moment and it nurtures me.

Responding to Extremist Behaviour

Today, seventy-six years ago Britain and France declared war on Germany as a result of the invasion of Poland two days earlier. The anniversary struck me as very relevant for today's times, with neo-Nazis marching in the United States. The British Prime Minister Neville Chamberlain is now forever known as the classic appeaser, the one who hesitated to declare war a year and more earlier when Hitler's forces were less powerful.

It's so easy in hindsight. If we declare war and it turns out to be a disaster we shout that our leaders were warmongers, trigger-happy or worse. Ask Tony Blair. If we don't react with military power and an aggressor then oppresses their own people or that of a neighbouring power, our political leaders are accused of standing by and allowing war crimes to be committed unchallenged.

So how does a person respond to the reality of neo-Nazis marching in America? What's the right response? Many people on Facebook, Twitter and the like respond in the words on many posters in the USA, with "Punch a Nazi" or similar unequivocal terms. In other words treat violence with violence. Does that merely inflame an already volatile situation? Does it allow people like President Trump to say there is violence "on many sides" and thus let off the hook behaviour that is unacceptable?

There are many armchair volunteers ready to conduct warfare online. Taunts and insults, one-sided evidence, simplistic single statements which try to suggest a coherent, comprehensive message.

The truth is that there is no way of knowing how to most effectively combat any perceived danger. He who hesitates is lost, says the wise old phrase. Look before you leap, counters another. History is great as a teacher in theory, much less so in real situations. Sometimes ignoring fascists makes the problem dwindle and the crisis disappears for a time. Other times it emboldens them to become more aggressive.

Mindfulness teaches us to notice as much as possible. From noticing we not only gain insights that life usually isn't as simple as some suggest, we also learn to question our own assumptions, biases and automatic reactions to events.

From that position of greater clarity and understanding we can make a decision about whether to become active in a cause, and if so, what sort of action we will take.

Mindfulness also teaches us to hesitate before jumping to responses. This is especially helpful on social media where knee-jerk reactions, rants, aggressive or unpleasant responses to messages are so common. There is also a trend common among men, and to a lesser extent women, to think that a wittier form of despising someone in a message is more acceptable than a blatant one. We are awash with machismo Scots on political matters.

What effect do most of these messages and counter-messages have? Hardening of attitudes on both sides most likely.

Mindfulness asks of us to be ultra-aware of how we make use of our time. Social media can be remarkably good and effective use of time but it is also so easy to waste bucket-loads of moments pursuing pointless temptations from celebrity gossip to a million opinions on whether Donald Trump is or is not likely to be indicted. Life goes by and we're not there. Life goes by and we're AWOL. Life goes by and we miss out on its wonderful diverse beauty because we are not in charge of our own wayward, flighty mind.

There are many people I know engaged in political activism who are more angry than effective, and more "against" than they are "for". Their minds are unhappy and unreceptive to life's joys but they cannot see this because they are so conditioned to think only in terms of what is wrong in society and the world.

The Buddha is reported in the classic Buddhist text The Dhammapada to have said "Hatred never ends through hatred. By non-hatred alone does it end." He then added "This is an ancient truth."

If the Buddha said it, this places his quote at around the fifth century before Christ, and even this long ago he is stated as saying that "hatred never ends through hatred" was already an ancient truth. Mindfulness helps us regain that truth.

Whether violence or non-violence is required to achieve or defend the kind of society we believe in, it will not be achieved by blinkered hatred and unthinking reactivity.

Tolerating Imperfection in Others

To Err is Human, To Forgive Divine. This quote is from the great English poet, Alexander Pope, though he used an ancient Latin phrase for the first part. I think it is one of the great statements in the English language. Lately, both on social media, and in everyday life, I have heard a plethora of harsh judgements about people who have said or done something wrong.

Recent examples have concerned two Conservative local councillors who had been found to make racist and sectarian comments online, and still more recently another Scottish Conservative who had implied very negative views about the Travelling communities of Scotland.

People were outraged when the two councillors, having been suspended, were allowed back to their normal roles and positions after pledging not to repeat their offensive views. Meanwhile people online urged the public to shout abuse at the Conservative who made the remark about the Travelling communities the next time he was in public. At his happens he is a professional football referee so he is probably used to being heckled in public.

Mindfulness has two components to it which are relevant to these scenarios. The first is empathy, the second reason, but they are intrinsically intertwined.

Why does someone say something hurtful about others in the first place? The answer at its most basic is simple, and universal. Genes and life experiences.

Nature and nurture. Things simply do not occur without prior cause. Everything in existence happens as part of a relentless series of chains of causes and effects. So the utterances of these politicians are simply the result of things that happened to them in the past mixed in with the unique genes they inherited from their parents.

Similarly the resultant outcry about their comments comes from another set of past experiences and the nudging of our genetic influences.

And in turn my genes and past experiences are telling me to write this article in response to the outcry. Here's why.

One of the things I see in Scotland is the unpleasant result of a huge amount of such causes and effects. Polarised opinions, loss of ability to stay calm and respectful while making points, the use vindictive words to try to cause maximum hurt. These things, while having causes in themselves, also result in harmful effects, a spiralling of vicious views and statements.

In this atmosphere some precious things get lost. Fellow feeling. Tolerance of difference of opinion. Acceptance that our side might not always be right.

And forgiveness.

If we never forgave ignorant or harmful words uttered by people and forced them out of office, there would be no one left on the planet to fill any post.

I'm not a religious person but Jesus put it brilliantly as he so often did.

"Let they who are without sin cast the first stone." and "Judge not, that ye be not judged.".

Those are salutary statements. We are all programmed. We are all imperfect. We are all prejudiced in some way. It is useful to remember this when we find our minds rising in a self-righteous way to condemn others' comments.

This doesn't mean we should accept hateful or bigoted statements, but the aim should be at the statements, not the people who say them.

Nor in my opinion should we scream "off with their heads" every time someone errs in this way. If we are to live peacefully in a society we not only have to learn to be more open, accepting and welcoming of different cultures and ways of thinking and being, we must also give people the opportunity to learn from their past errors and continue to play important roles in society.

So next time you feel the urge to pontificate and shout "Resign!" just take a deep breath, allow that mental space to remind you that you too, are not exactly perfect, and then consider what response you could create that states a clear opinion but seeks at the same time to unify and allow a chance for redemption.

It is so easy to rabble-rouse. The baying of the mob is not the prettiest part of our species' history.

It's a lot harder to lower tensions and nurture peace but ultimately that's what the vast majority of people in any society want.

Gratitude

Today is an important date in my family's life. Seventy-eight years ago on this day, 17 September 1939, the Soviet Red Army marched into eastern Poland, almost unopposed, because the Polish army were at that time desperately trying to stop the German army which had invaded two weeks earlier from the west.

My father had just turned seventeen, his younger sisters were fourteen and twelve, and his father and mother in their mid-forties and mid-thirties respectively. They lived in the eastern part of pre-war Poland, called the Kresy or borderlands, which is now in western Ukraine.

That same day the Red Army rolled into their little farming village. The whole community was in a state of shock. As the day turned into early evening there was a knock on the farmhouse door. My grandfather, Wladyslaw opened it. A Jewish friend was there, looking afraid.

"The Russians have pulled together a list of potential trouble-makers who might lead any resistance to their authority. And you're one of them. The order is to find the people on the list and execute them immediately."
This friend was a member of the then-banned communist party in Poland. Yet he had risked his life to warn Wladyslaw, a Catholic anti-communist.

Wladyslaw had in recent years been harassed for his pluralist views by the immediate pre-war ruling party in Poland, which was far-right and anti-Semitic, so he was respected by the various local ethnic minorities but not be extremists on all sides.

While pondering this warning with his family and discussing what options they had, there came another knock at the door. Everyone froze. Was it the Soviet hit squad? Wladyslaw went to the door. It was another friend. This time a Ukrainian. Many Ukrainians had wanted but failed to get independence after World War One, and there was a campaign of violence towards Poles by some militia groups. Wladyslaw had mediated in several disputes, so was well-known by all local Ukrainians.

The Ukrainian confirmed the Jew's warning and added that the Red Army and some local Ukrainian allies were on their way to the Stepeks' home. If Waldyslaw didn't leave right now, he would not make the next day alive.
The Ukrainian personally took Wladyslaw in his cart westwards to the nearest train station where Wladyslaw could try and make his way to his relatives in the south.

Through the acts of kindness and courage, and placing humanity above tribal loyalties, my grandfather survived for almost another four years, as head of a local resistance unit fighting the Nazi forces in the area. The Jewish friend almost certainly died in the Holocaust, and the Ukrainian friend was arrested on his way back to his home, imprisoned and only narrowly escaped execution for being suspected of aiding Wladyslaw.

We all have many people to whom we owe much, even our lives. Midwives, doctors, nurses, teachers, parents, amongst the most obvious. But also the unrecognised. The people who sweep out streets, empty of bins, keep our public parks and roadsides maintained. The folk who maintain reservoirs, pipelines, water purification plants.

We have so much to be grateful for, and so many to whom we owe gratitude. Mindfulness recognises this through ongoing subtle, gentle, clear awareness. The green tea I take in the morning required hundreds of people to get it from the bush the leaves grew on until it reached the person at the till who scanned it and let me put it in my shopping bag. I make sure it's Fairtrade so that I don't inadvertently support exploitation of labour.

It's all about clear thinking. The clearer we think the better the decisions we make. The better the decisions the better our lives will be, and the lives of those around us, all else being equal. And we can deliberately develop clearer thinking by practising moment by moment. Simply observation and awareness of the breath for example. Right now, notice your in-breath, its coolness, its freshness, the way the lungs fill and feel strong. Notice the out-breath, its slow measured release, the deflation of the lungs, and the sense of quiet peace as the now warm air leaves your nostrils. This is true mental development. Five senses, an observant mind, and an opportunity to practise it at every moment.

Conditioned

Most people are on the road to nowhere. Like everyone else they got a set of genes from their parents that not only made them look the way they do, but to a greater or lesser extent, made them think and react the way they do. It's a complicated subject but when you add in the ingredient of all of life experiences it doesn't take a genius to realise that between these genes and these life experiences, who we are and how we think and react is a result of that messy, labyrinthine concoction.

Where do you fit into this series on influences on who you have become? In fact, let's go back one step, what do you actually mean by who you are? We think of ourselves as "me", a pretty stable personality, albeit with the odd ups and downs, and maybe occasionally an uncharacteristic outburst for good or bad. So a kind of solid, fixed thing, but with blips.

This is the "me" the Buddha looked at in the fabled days leading up to what is called his enlightenment or state of nirvana. When he just sat there day in day out, only stopping to eat and drink when necessary, he had a remarkable insight. This thing he called "me" didn't really seem to be a thing at all. It was a process, or flow as he put it. A never-ending flow of shifts and change, of flux and movement, especially of the mind. When he tried to locate a stable "me" or self he discovered that he couldn't find one. All that existed was this stream of thoughts, emotions, reactions, ideas, moods and mental states.

Moreover he had the great insight that this "me" that he couldn't even find wasn't in charge of what was pulsing out of his mind. It was all automatic. As another great Buddhist teacher put it "there is no thinker behind the thought".

Now that's challenging stuff to read on a hopefully otherwise relaxing Sunday for you. The bad news is it gets worse. Not only does there not seem to be a "me", in other words "you" but this whole stream of thoughts and feelings that just pour out of your brain and take you over from moment to moment wasn't chosen by you either.

So whether you're a top notch lawyer, the First Minister, a retired ex-plumber or the world's most expensive player Neymar, you probably had pretty little say in how you got to be where you are. Your automatic brain, your genetic tendencies, and the series of manifold experiences, coincidences, and good and bad luck led you to where you are now. Even the supposedly reasoned major life choices you made were for the most part made for you, or at least hugely influenced by factors outwith your control.

So to the two big things in life according to conventional society.

Career. You didn't take into account over 90% of all the careers you could have chosen because your genes and life experiences didn't introduce them to your frame of reference.

Love of your life. You didn't happen to meet 99.99% of all the choices of partner, husband, wife, so your genes tricked you into sexual and relationship attraction, made you fall head over heels in love, which is pretty close to a form of temporary insanity, and boom, decision made.

So, if the dice had rolled even just slightly differently you'd currently be doing an entirely different career, or being a stay at home non-working adult, and go home to an entirely different partner, possibly of the other sex, or to no partner at all.

Mindfulness is as close to an intervention in this morass as we can find. We learn to notice this strange state of affairs as pretty accurate, no matter how bizarre it seems. And, accepting this reality, we try to do what we can to bring at least some bearing to the arrangement.

By developing our skill of noticing what's going on in each moment, we can see that certain thoughts and responses that arise in our mind are not helpful, and let them go. We can then see if a better alternative pops up and if it does, do that instead. That's it. Do it during as many moments as you can. You'll be amazed at how it changes the direction of your life in the long run. You're still conditioned but significantly less so than in the past, and that makes all the difference.

Choice or No Choice Now

30 days hath September. All gone now. October already. It'll be Christmas before we know it. Where does it all go?

We all have thoughts like this, and as we get older, we think the decades have gone by like months of the year. For people of my generation any song after about 1990 is recent. Our life looking forwards seems to stretch on forever, though we know it doesn't, while the past seemed to get compressed into a small tight package, even though we know that's nonsense.

What we have is always only one thing. Now. The Present. This Moment. And whatever we call it, it's only located in one place. Here. Or as the great doctor and pioneering mindfulness researcher Jon Kabat-Zinn titled it in one of his many superb books, Wherever You Go, There You Are.

So, Here. And Now. An opportunity to pay attention and perceive or create what's possible. My first teacher of mindfulness, a Tibetan Buddhist monk, once said "Reality is a field of potential".

For me this explains how to do life. Reality is Life therefore "Life is a field of potential". You only experience life in the present moment. So each moment is a field of potential.

Let's look at an example.

Someone behind you at a roundabout anticipates you setting off, but you decide you can't go out yet. The driver of the car behind you bumps into your car. You're already on edge as the traffic's been slow and you might be late for a meeting. There's no major damage but a wee scratch so you have to exchange insurance details.

Your mind is thinking – and because this is a respectable Sunday newspaper I won't say all the swear words going on in your head, but you know there is a whole stream of them. "… idiot", "should have been looking where he was… going", "wasting my… time" are all emerging from your mind in a stream of petulance, anger, frustration and impatience.

Alternatively, the accident happens. You notice with mindfulness the annoyance and irritation that your mind has created automatically without your consent, and choose deliberately and quietly to let those unhelpful emotions go. This takes about ten seconds, aided by you focussing on your breath, slowly, cool and fresh with the in-breath, then warm and peaceful as it flows gently back out.

Mind clear, you realise that although you might now be late, you can't do anything about that. It's therefore irrelevant. The driver apologises and to ease his discomfort when he apologises you say "Don't worry, these things happen. Let's leave it to the insurance folk". He's grateful you're calm about it.

"Reality is a field of potential." Your life in that moment had an infinite array of possible options, and of the two we have described, the automatic reaction would unpleasantly affect your mood for much of the day, with the ripples of your lingering annoyance causing a negative mood amongst the colleagues in your workplace. Moreover your mind registered yet another bout of negative emotions, and as a result has strengthened that habit as your preferred way to react in future. Oh, and you've probably taken a few seconds off your life expectancy.

The other choice means that your mood would be unaffected by the time you got to work, there would be no negative ripples pulsing out and affecting your colleagues; there might even be some positive ripples going out because you feel good about how well you handed a potentially irritating experience. Meanwhile in the constantly neuroplastic world of the mind, your mind has been reshaped by your constructive and skilful response, and is learning to strengthen that mindfulness skill of noticing, and the subsequent skill of letting negative emotions dissipate by observing them or deflecting them with observation of the breath. This means you'll probably be more able to do similar in future, you'll have weakened your habit of getting annoyed so easily, and you'll live a few seconds longer as a direct result.

The Buddha said "The wise person, as if holding a set of scales, chooses what is good and avoids what is destructive." Learn to be a wise person.

Living with Uncertainty

There's a famous story in the Chinese classical work of philosophy, The Book of Chuang Tzu, where the author tells us he has just awoken from a dream in which he was a butterfly. But then he ponders this happening and reflects that he can't say for sure whether that was indeed the reality, or whether he was in fact a butterfly dreaming he was now Chuang Tzu.

This story had played out in science fiction films like The Matrix and it can ultimately be headache-inducing because there's actually no way of knowing for certain which alternate version is the real one. Of course we all have real fanatical friends who would be quick to tell us that in fact there might be a trillion alternate universes, in one of which Chuang Tzu would in fact be the butterfly.

Pondering such unknowables can be fun for some of us. The problem is that we often get totally wound up by more serious unknowables or uncertainties in life. Take Brexit for example. Try to leave aside your political view of it just now.

OK, I realise that's impossible for you so just pretend for a moment.

There is in fact no way of knowing for certain what the impact of Brexit will be. Before you rush in to disagree, consider these points.

Impact on whom? Britain? Scotland? South Lanarkshire, where I live, Hamilton, the town in South Lanarkshire where I live? Me personally? With or without my family?

And for how long are we talking about this measured impact? The first three years? Thirty years? Till 2100? Till the next millennium?

Even if we agree on the who and the how long, doesn't it depend on the precise details of the negotiations, of which we don't yet know the outcome? Also the overall global economic growth figures over the next few years? Or the specific deals Britain might be able to do with other countries? Not to mention the possibility of a second Indy referendum, which if the result was Yes, would presumably affect Scotland's impact, the rest of the UK's impact, and the impact on the EU, which would also depend on whether Scotland stayed in, was out, or was out but negotiating to rejoin the EU?

Now this is just basic stuff. Truly complex stuff is how your mind works. How you respond to different situations. How you cope with illness, deaths, job issues, ageing, family and friendship ups and downs, and so on. These are all unknowables until they hit you.

And yet we fret over them endlessly just like we do with Brexit, and just as poor old Chuang Tzu was doing about whether he was a human or a highly sophisticated butterfly capable of dreaming he was an ancient Taoist philosopher.

Another ancient philosopher, Gautama Siddhartha, better known to us as the Buddha, had very clear views on how we waste so much time and energy on continually ruminating and debating what is not knowable. "The Buddha" means the awakened one, and I think he was exceptionally awake when he made the following observation.

Continuing to debate something you can't actually find a definite answer to leads to "a wilderness of opinions". This is such a noble truth. While we're interminably debating, with others or just inside to yourself, the full potential of this wonderful life just slips away moment by moment by moment. Over a lifetime we can throw away literally decades on pointless ponderings and ruminations.

Take an extreme example. Suppose you have terminal cancer. What is better use of your time, to literally wake up and smell the roses, or to wake up and wonder if today will be the day you die? We all do little versions of this every day, by getting upset and way out of proportion over trivial things. Meanwhile the smell of the roses wafts by unnoticed, and a hundred moments of your life is lost forever.

Be mindful. Learn to pay attention to your thoughts, moods, reactions and your five senses. Learn to let go, gently, without fuss or rancour, of the rubbish and the poison. It doesn't matter if you never know whether you were in fact a human or a butterfly. What matters is you have awareness of being alive. Use it fully because it doesn't last forever.

Change

We like stability, except when we don't. Change is fine when we are the ones deciding to make things a bit different. But when change is forced upon us by others or by external events, we react negatively.

We live in a bubble, a delusion that things will stay more or less the same, at least for long periods of time. But both history and common sense tells us this is unbelievably naive.

A friend wrote to me recently about the state of the world. She said she felt this was, as Dickens put it, "the worst of times". She cited Brexit, the police brutality in Catalonia, and the mass shooting in Las Vegas.

I replied pointing out that in our childhood in the sixties we had the Cuban crisis, Vietnam, Biafra, Rhodesia's apartheid regime, the assassinations of JFK, MLK, and Robert Kennedy, and at the end of that decade, the shooting dead by US military of four students in Ohio.

At a more mundane level change comes in many guises. We get sick, ill, require an operation. People we love get cancer. Relationships break up painfully. People we know die unexpectedly.

Change happens. Life is change. You are a flow of non-stop changes.

This has been a key message of three great philosophical civilisations of ancient times, all amazingly at roughly the same time, though thousands of miles from each another. In Ephesus in the 5th century BC the Greek philosopher Heraclitus taught the "no man steps into the same river twice". Meanwhile in present-day Nepal and northern India, Gautama Siddhartha, soon to become known to the world as Buddha (the awakened one) taught that we are not stable solid selves, nor do we have immortal souls, but are, rather, more like a river, just as Heraclitus alluded to, a flow or constant shift, flux and change. And further east yet again, in China, the unknown author or authors of the Tao te Ching, though said to be written by the mythical Lao Tzu, explained that the entire universe is a flow, called Tao.

Although all three had different reasons for trying to bring this to the attention of humans in their own time, and differed in their interpretation of what to do about the reality of this highly scientific notion that everything is in flux and flow, they all agreed on one thing; we should realise that this is the case. We are not stable, fixed, unchanging. Nor is the world around us.

Get this deeply into our thick skulls, they were saying, because if you don't you are going to be hit by every single bit of bad news, personal or global, that comes your way. You'll no soon recover from one storm than another comes along and blows all your healing to bits again.

Mindfulness was deliberately devised as a tool of liberating yourself from such an unstable way of living and being. Gautama, the Buddha, worked it out for himself. If your mind gets knocked from pillar to post by not just all the truly awful things in life, but also, because we are petty little toddlers at heart, wanting everything to go our own way, then you better get in control of that mind, and the sooner the better.

Who is driving the bus? Donald Trump? Teresa May? The United Nations? The weather? A lone gunman shooting out at a crowd from a hotel window? The Taoists, the Buddha, and Heraclitus will tell you if you are wise enough to read their classic texts, just as scientists have told us for centuries now, that it's all cause and effect. We blame the latest bad guy or woman but we don't see that they are also the result of earlier events, and so on back in time forever. This is the way of change. It is relentless.

Notice clearly and calmly with mindfulness. Let go of useless or harmful mental reactions that arise in your head. Don't be the cause of negative ripples streaming into the world just because you can't control your emotions, your thoughts, your words. Try to be the cause, the catalyst of constructive influences, flows, ripples in this world. That's all we can do; stop being a producer of negative causes and effects, and try where possible to be the creator of helpful ones.

Moulding your Mind

So it's that time of year again for me. You'll have yours too. The dates that make you remember. For some people it's Christmas. If you've lost family then Christmas can be a time you dread because all the grief, the loss, and the plain stark fact of them not being there, can weigh you down for weeks before the 25th December.

For me it's a four week period starting in a few days' time. On Wednesday 25th it's the 75th anniversary of my grandmother's death in Teheran, and the following day, 26th October, is the fifth anniversary of my father's death. Just over three weeks' later it's the anniversary of the date my mother died, also five years ago. That they died only three weeks' apart means that I remember both of them for the whole of this period of the year. My mind can't separate out their deaths as two events. It's one stretched chunk of time, a blur of woe, and memories of being washed over by emotions while organising funerals, eulogies to be prepared, paperwork, and trying to ensure that my children were handling the death of both their remaining grandparents.

The deaths of my parents was real. I saw the decline then the absence of life in each of what were once living bodies.

The death of my grandmother Janina however, is different, I never knew her. I decided to deliberately invent her life afresh, to cultivate and nourish her in me.

She was forty when she died, of starvation and exhaustion, in what we'd now call a refugee hospital in Persia, now Iran. Two months earlier she had finally been evacuated from the Soviet Union, one of tens of thousands of survivors from massive ethnical cleansings in eastern Poland by Stalin's troops in early 1940. Deported with her were my father and his two younger sisters. They were teenagers.

On release from their labour camp in late 1941 they had to make their own way from near the Arctic Circle to what is now Uzbekistan, and having no money and little food, they frequently got lost of stuck in the feet of snow in Siberia. Thus by the time of their final voyage to freedom across the Caspian Sea in August 1941 they had been wanderers and internal refugees in the Soviet Union for almost a year, most of which time they suffered malnutrition and fatigue.

I knew little of this until I started practising mindfulness, and I have used my mindfulness since to deliberately learn as much about Janina as I could, not only to try to know her in retrospect, but to cultivate inside my mind a more universal sense of compassion and empathy for others. Not just other people, but all forms of life.

Every time I drink water I bring her to mind. Every time. A woman who died in large part for the want of water on their odyssey to freedom. Her organs started to malfunction for the lack of water. Every sip a cultivation of compassion.

Every sip a nurturing of a determination to do what I can to help change the culture of humanity so that it makes it truly unacceptable that living sentient beings can be subjected to such agonies.

I do this because I know that compassion and kindness are the finest of human values. I do it because not to do so means I will treat others' pain with less empathy and practical assistance than I otherwise could have felt and done.

At a scientific level this is me deliberately using my understanding that our mind is neuroplastic. That means that every experience we have changes our brain and therefore changes who we are. My mindfulness practice of experiencing compassion at my grandmother's unbearably awful death creates a drip by drip growth of love and kindness for all life in my mind. I become, thought by thought, reflection by reflection, a better human being. Literally.

As for my parents' deaths, I think back. I let healing healthy grief flow, then gently turn it into an avalanche of gratitude for all they did for me. I turn grief to joy.

This is how I mindfully use and deal with this time of the year.

Change of Culture in Organisations

Many people who read this column will have experience of work-related events. I'm frequently asked to do talks on various subjects, nowadays mostly mindfulness, at training days or conferences for leaders or senior managers of business and non-profit organisations. I try to attend as much of the event as possible, in order to get a feel for the atmosphere, the people attending, and most importantly the culture that seems to fill the room, before I take to the floor.

These events vary enormously. Some are formal and quite staid. Others are self-consciously informal, as if all attending have been firmly instructed that they must be relaxed. And some have a natural and genuinely open feel.

Even before I started teaching mindfulness in 2004 I used to go to such events in my business and social enterprise careers. A lot of the contributions were very practical, helping people to understand the latest situation in a particular field of interest, or how to improve skills in a certain area of expertise. But some are stilted, as if the speaker had just learned their content from a book, and were now parroting it word for word, with no sense that they had ever lived the messages they were sharing with those attending.

I often wonder what happens to individuals and organisations after an event. There are many professional "motivational" speakers whose task is to give people a jolt or spark a determination to change their life or their organisation.

169

Some I have found to be authentic and inspiring, others sadly glib and shallow, more showbiz than insightful.

What happens after these events? The combination of busyness at work and home, and the claustrophobic power of the old habitual ways we do things in the office, quickly force out all of our newly-created energy and determination to change things. Soon the event becomes just another vague memory, one of a hundred you've attended, been inspired or motivated by, only to find there was no lasting effect.

Yet we absolutely need radical transformations in our workplaces, whether private, public or third sector. It is all about the culture, nothing else. You can tell the moment you walk into a building or a room whether this is a happy place to work in, whether you can be human, warm, kind, joyful, or whether there's a cold so-called professional atmosphere, where no one can breathe freely till they leave for home.

Predictably I'd call for a culture of mindfulness in every workplace, as in every home. As in every individual's mind. The research findings over almost forty years have shown that being truly mindful brings the following benefits to individuals and therefore ultimately to the culture of the places they work.

Greater sense of contentment, and ability to handle knee-jerk emotional reactions to situations.

A sense of relaxed calmness, even when the proverbial hits the fan, when calmness is most needed.

Increased clarity of thinking, so better, and more inclusive decisions are made, for the benefit of the organisation, and all involved.

A higher degree of attention and sustained focus, combined with a lighter sense of mind, meaning that we get more done, at a better quality, with less fatigue.

Finally, and most importantly, a sharp rise in our sense of compassion for the suffering of others, and in altruism, the desire to help others without seeking selfish return. This is so needed in the private sector, where the common refrain "we're not a charity" sinks everyone's spirits, employees, customers, and suppliers.

Unless and until organisations and especially their leaders, recognise this, all their fancy, well-meant, and heartfelt conferences and workshops and training and inspirational talks will be ninety percent a waste of time and money.

To paraphrase Tony Blair, our three long-term priorities in work has to be culture, culture, and culture. Without the right culture you can still be successful but it will be a shadowy success, bringing unnecessary misery and boredom to your colleagues, and a sense of absence of trust to society as a whole.

A mindfulness culture, one which deliberately and continually develops contentment, clarity, calmness and compassion, is the greatest success any organisation can accomplish.

Sound

Music is the most mysterious thing in human culture. How can a series of sounds, without lyrics, move you to tears, lift you to joy? It's just vibrations that travel through air. We evolved over millions of years to have ears and a brain that, together, transform these vibrations into what we call sounds.

I was at a concert recently, seeing for the second time in a year the astonishing Roy Wood, the founder of The Move, ELO, and Wizzard, and composer of probably the most played Christmas song of all time, I Wish it Could Be Christmas Every Day. In my biased opinion he is one of the greatest songwriters of his generation, massively underestimated.

The audience were all long-time fans, knew every song, and sang along from start to finish. Such happiness.

Such mindfulness. In two ways.

Almost everyone there had every song memorised in their heads, both the tunes and the lyrics. It takes a lot of practice to memorise something but once there it lasts for decades, maybe a lifetime. We all have hundreds of complete songs in our brains ready to come out at a moment's notice. This is an example of unintentional mindfulness; we learn something by heart through repeated pure attention.

The second way was the pure mindfulness on the night. Full attention was given to the performances of the songs. No distractions, no television on it the background, no mobile phones unless to take a quick snap of the band. It is rare for us to give such undivided attention for so long, and when we do we reap much greater rewards at each and every moment. A Harvard University study from 2014 showed the on average our mind wanders 47% of our waking day.

Seeing joy and happiness in a large group of people is a very rare thing. We are not often amongst large groups in a relatively small space so that is unusual in itself. Secondly, expressions of joy and overt happiness are not the norm in human everyday experience. This was untainted joy unlike, for example, when we see mass celebrations in sport, where there is always a loser, and sometimes in football stadia the most distinct emotion is derision aimed at the losing team's fans than celebrating our own team.

Yet listening to music when you are alone is sometimes more profoundly affecting, in a completely different way. Now you're not sharing with anyone else. It is deeply personal and inner.

I have a very obscure CD called Shakuhachi – The Japanese Flute. It comprises five pieces, lasting from almost four minutes to nine and a half. I can't call them songs.

Mood music may be as close as we have in English to describing these pieces, but the individual notes are at times so long that it's more like the wind than a sound from an instrument (the Shakuhachi is a Japanese flute or sorts). Some of the pieces are centuries old, thought to be composed as aids to meditative practices. I find listening to it entrancing, almost literally, yet it's not music, nor is it the sounds of nature.

But nothing beats silence. Or quietness to be more precise. When the outside world is quiet, and the mind is still, and the emotions calmed and at peace, something remarkable can arise. Perfect inner tranquillity and contentment. It is difficult to put into words how this feels, nor how restorative it is in terms of destressing, revitalising, uplifting. It's like being a rechargeable battery and feeling that you have been plugged in, and you feel the life energy inside you slowly return. In a non-mystical sense it really is like being reborn, like coming back from the form of mental death we experience when we are weary.

I was taught mindfulness by a brilliant teacher. He told me that any time I experienced something unusual in my practices, not to get excited or try to understand it. Rather I had to just keep practising.

This is how I feel about my relationship to music. I understand a wee bit of the science now but the mystery, joy, awe that it can bring, I am happy just to experience and absorb, and don't care why music, sound, silence are magical. Mindfulness just notes that they are, and celebrates this moment by moment as this unfolds.

The C Word and Mindfulness

An area where mindfulness has proven to be of immense value is for people suffering from major illnesses, and for their families too. Not that mindfulness can in any way cure physical conditions, but it can help enormously how we react to having such ailments, or help us handle our emotions about people we love who have serious or life-long illnesses.

Cancer is the biggie. It creates in us such a momentous fear that we hesitate to even use the word in conversation, especially when we're with someone who suffers from it. My mother died of it. Coincidentally the fifth anniversary of her death is six days after this article in due to be published in this newspaper. My sister has had cancer for eight years now, saved and supported by what was at first unproven experimental drugs. She was too unwell to go to mum's funeral. How ironic a situation, to be unable to attend the funeral of the person you loved so much, who died of the same disease that prevents you from attending.

As Maya Angelou put it so eloquently, so powerfully, Still I Rise. Or rather, still they rise, those people who suffer cancer. It is astonishing to see the resilience, the ability to face the fears, the pain, the sense of drift and dissolution.

But not everyone handles cancer equally well, and often the loved ones and carers for those suffering find themselves confused and lost under the weight of emotions and fatigue that go with caring and loving and fearing and anger at the world and at life itself.

175

I was asked to speak on mindfulness and cancer at the annual Kidney Cancer Information Day last Wednesday. How can someone who has never had cancer talk to those who have had or still have it? I can't share my experience of it.

However I can share a few things. The most important is compassion. Along with love. It's strange to put it in writing like this, but we can nurture love and compassion in ourselves, deliberately, slowly, continually, patiently. Love for all life. Love for all people. Love even for those we don't like. Love even for those we feel are ruining the world or putting it in danger, such as some major political leaders.

We can develop love, empathy, compassion and other emotions essential to good relationships purely by repetitively and creatively bringing them to our attention regularly. As great contemporary psychologist wrote, happiness is allocation of attention. In other words where we place our minds most, that's what will grow inside us. So be careful about what you think about or do. This is the neuroplastic nature of the mind. It is shaped and reshaped time and again by experiences we have.

Why would we do this? Positive qualities such a love, compassion, and kindness are not only appreciated by those around us when we show these emotions. They also nurture our own physical and mental health.

A fascinating series of studies have shown that negative emotions and states of mind appear to accelerate aging and physical deterioration. At the same time each expression of a negative emotion shapes the mind in the exact same way as the positive ones do, as explained earlier. So whenever we are angry, sad, depressed, anxious – all common experiences of people suffering from cancer, or indeed their families – we are strengthening's the mind's tendency to experience those traits again in the future.

As an antidote of sorts we can therefore train and develop helpful qualities of mind and skilled techniques for people who suffer from cancer, or whose loved ones struggle with the reality of this disease. Handling anxiety is one such skill. Letting go of unhelpful worries is another. Nurturing the awareness required to sense the beauty and joy of being alive and of life outside our window is yet another.

If we can strengthen these qualities of mind we can still enjoy and love the moments in our day even as we know deep inside that we are seriously unwell. The two are not incompatible. As the wonderful Thich Nhat Nanh put it, happiness is too important in life to wait until we are happy in order to experience it. Shape your mind. Don't let cancer or any other major condition in your life dictate how you feel about being alive. You can be in charge.

Ripples

The core scientific basis of mindfulness is neuroplasticity. Although the idea was suggested by many scientists and thinkers the term was coined by Polish neurophysiologist Jerzy Konorski in the middle of the twentieth century. It's probably the most important think most people don't know about themselves.

It means that your way of thinking, reacting, and behaving is subject to change at any and at all times. This happens through primarily external events. In everyday terms we can think of it as ongoing cause and effect. Someone says something unpleasant about us and we become sad. We think of this as a one-off incident, it happened, now it's gone. But in fact the experience has embedded in your brain and in some subtle, unconscious way, changed you. It may be that you now like that person a little less, or you feel a tiny bit less confident about the subject of the remark. The ultimate effect is that you are now a different you as a result of a single remark.

This flow and flux of causes and effects, ripples that bump into you as life experiences, has been happening to you since the moment your brain started to function before you were born. It's still happening. You're being affected by the very fact of reading this column.

But ripples aren't things that just happen to you and to everyone else. They are also created in turn by each of us. Every single thing you either think, feel emotionally, say, write or do causes effects, ripples.

Some of these ripples affect only ourselves. So a pleasant thought about nice the weather is on a cold but clear and sunny winter's morning is not only produced in our mind but the very fact of it being produced itself affects your mind for the future. All the other forms of activity you do usually affect other people, including even our involuntary facial expressions.

What does this tell us? That we're susceptible to change even if we don't want to be, and moreover we are susceptible to harmful or unhelpful forms of change even without our awareness that this is actually happening. It also tells us that we capable, wittingly or not, of hurting other people and changing how they perceive life, themselves, others.

Given that this can and does happen in virtually every single moment, let's look at some extreme examples. John Lennon walks out of his apartment door, a man walks up to him smiling, and shoots him dead. Imagine a tiny change to that scenario. John Lennon walks out of his apartment door, a man walks up to him smiling, and decides not to shoot him dead. Lennon goes on to compose songs which we are not able to imagine because he never did get the chance to write them.

Even more extreme. Archduke Franz Ferdinand of Austria is assassinated in June 1914. A month later Austria-Hungary declares war on Serbia. Four years later forty million people have been killed as a direct result of that decision to declare war.

Other direct effects are: Russia has had a world-changing revolution leading to the first communist state, the Austrian and German empires have been destroyed, Poland re-emerges and Czechoslovakia is created. The further ramifications of this war leads to the Second World War in 1939.

What if the Austrians decided not to go to war but instead to try to build bridges with Serbia? We can't know the effects but for hundreds of millions of people over the next century a different fate would have resulted. All because of one decision.

This is why mindfulness matters so very much and why in my view everyone should learn to practise it. It enables one to have a much better chance of noticing what's going on in each moment. The more aware we are of the potential of external effects on who we are, the better chance we have or gently letting them fall away without the effect on us becoming a reality. And the more aware we are of our own thoughts, moods, feelings and impulses, the more likely we'll be of perceiving that certain ones are destructive or hurtful, and from that insight let drop what might otherwise have caused a poisonous ripple into our mind or into the world and the people around us.

Our mindful responses may not prevent two world wars or save the life of a great songwriter and performer, but they may help you not become a less happy version of yourself and may help you make someone's day brighter rather than darker.

Mindfulness and Power

I attended a half-day event on Power, Health and Social Justice hosted by the ever-excellent Glasgow Centre for Population Health. The subject of power, who wields it, who is excluded, and the consequences of power and powerlessness is hugely important. It affects how every one of us fares in life, and how our society feels as a whole.

It's impossible to attempt to cover the whole of this subject in this column so here instead are just a few reflections.

Mindfulness-trained leaders would be nurtured in clarity of thought, calmness, contentment, and compassion. This is what mindfulness brings. How many of our elected leaders and representatives are sufficiently clear-thinking, calm, content and compassionate? How many of our business leaders? And you?

A compassionate leader would want all citizens to feel confident and engaged enough to make their voice heard in their community and in their country. A clear-thinking leader would work to make that a reality. They would act to ensure that all citizens feel not only able to access the temples of power, but know they can contribute once they're there. How many of our people feel completely excluded, unable to reach those who might make a difference?

From a mindfulness perspective there can be no such thing as real democracy. Democracy means the power of the people; but people never unanimously agree. What we mean by democracy is voting in an election or referendum, whereby a majority get some version of what they want while the minority get what they expressly didn't want. That is not people power, that is dictatorship of the majority. I'm not arguing against it or suggesting a better system; merely stating that we should use the correct words when describing things. This is not only semantics. If democracy is not possible then a clear, calm mindful voice tells us we should say that, then go on to explore how power should best be granted to a person or group, and under what conditions and for how long. In other words we need to deeply review our constitution to find better ways of sharing formal power.

There's a much deeper aspect to this question of power and public health. It's not only our official leaders who need to be trained to be profoundly mindful; it's all of us. If we, the electorate are not trained to understand how conditioned we are, how biased, how prejudiced, how literally ignorant of issues, and then taught how to manage and overcome these deluded views, then we do, as the old phrase puts it, get the government we deserve.

We see this this absence of mindfulness through history of revolutions. Old regimes are overthrown, utopias are promised, then what follows are millions on the guillotine, in the Gulag, in the gas chambers, in killing fields.

Power is a very heavy, dangerous tool. The people who wield it need to have the mental strength to bear such a weight lightly, calmly, gently. And most of us are not equipped by life alone or our genes to be this way naturally.

We know so many abuses of power. In our governments and parliaments, in our churches and institutions, in small businesses and global corporations. Also in our homes, our schools, our streets. The saying goes "power corrupts" but in fact most of us carry the seeds of this corruption in our minds, through that mysterious combination of DNA and life experiences.

I stepped down as Convenor of Council for the Scottish Green Party in 2004. It was the highest position in a party that is instinctively wary of putting power and "leadership" into one or a few hands. I did so because I felt I needed to work more on the cultivation of my own mental qualities through my mindfulness practices before I'd be fit to take anything like that role in future. More than a decade later I'm still working at it, and still not yet fit.

So where does that leave me upon reflection? Empower yourself by starting to take full control of the thoughts and reactions that are produced by your own mind. Only when we are capable of that, and therefore able to stop the destructive elements of our mind's relentless production line, can we be truly fit for positions of power of any sort. Only then will we nurture something of the intelligence, wisdom and compassion to review our totally dysfunctional levels of power inequalities and make a better set of systems for the good of all.

Malleable Minds

After the death of my mother five years ago, three weeks after the death of my father, at her funeral I greeted the Polish priest Father Marian, at the doorway of St. Mary's church in Hamilton.

"We are now both orphans" he said.

Boom! He had explained everything in just five words. Bereft of my parents. Living without their continued existence alongside me. And his word "both", an expression of solidarity, that word "Solidarity" which for Poland means so much more than just working together.

It was while reading Carol Craig's remarkable new book "Hiding in Plain Sight" that this memory and the corresponding emotions, came back to me. The book is about Adverse Childhood Experiences (ACE) and how they may explain Scotland's disproportionate scale of physical and mental health issues, and some of our social and behavioural problems. I wholeheartedly recommend the book, and think it gives us a solid perspective from which to work to make our country, our communities, and our fellow Scots make progress from wherever we are in our inner lives to somewhere much healthier and kinder.

The book made me reflect on two things with mindfulness.

The first was that my upbringing was quite unique. Many of the stories Carol shares in the book I fully recognised, but not about my own life, but about my friends from primary school. Dads down the pub on a Friday night. Mums "skelping" my friends in public. And, unrelated to parents but universal in my generation, teachers belting pupils for "misdemeanours" such as getting a sum wrong or being late for class. It wasn't all gloom for my friends, nor gloomy at all for some, but for most there were frequent experiences that we would now consider barbaric. These are ACE and they affect who we have become.

But my father wasn't Scottish. He was Polish. He had been brutalised to a degree none of us could imagine. He saw his mother beaten and broken, his young sisters threatened with guns. He had had a rifle put to his head on several successive days. He lived in fear of imminent starvation or death from thirst. This was in his late teenage years, and though he was as a result often a difficult father and though my brothers, sisters and I undoubtedly experienced ACE, they were of a different order, and a much less substantial scale than most of those shared in Carol's book. My mindful thought was how on Earth my father managed to function at all, let alone as a good, humane, kind-hearted father and citizen. It says an enormous amount about him as a person, and about the human spirit, our ability to recover and succeed in life despite mind-boggling suffering.

The second insight Carol's book gave me was about mindfulness itself, which is mentioned at the end of the book as one of many techniques that can help people who have suffered ACE. Mindfulness, practised in its original form as part of a deep, whole life philosophy and way of being, rather than a mechanical method sometimes now taught, starts with the assumption that we are all in some way not quite right. There runs through us a vein of dissatisfaction, frustration, an inability to be at peace and feel content. This can only come from our genes together with our life experiences. ACE are a major part of this, and we have all had some degree of adverse childhood experiences, because no one's upbringing was perfect.

ACE arise because the mind is malleable. It is shaped and changed by our every experience. Childhood matters most because that's when the brain most absorbs life experiences in order for us to become functioning beings. But the key message for me, and I hope for you, is that, no matter where you are mentally, and whatever caused you to be what you are, you can still change. You can learn to cope, and from there learn to prevent new negative traits. You can learn to nurture the most humane, loving and creative qualities of the human mind. Love, compassion, kindness and joy are possible for us. This is the direction of travel Scotland must take, and practising mindfulness will be a significant aid on that long path to social sanity and happiness.

Once in Royal David's City

So tomorrow is Christmas, the day chosen to celebrate the birth of Jesus. I want to remind you of this, because most people don't think about it during the days up to, and including Christmas Day. Christmas has come to mean, for most of us, a time to get together with family and give gifts to each other. Essentially it's a celebration of family, and that is a great thing.

I'm not Christian, nor a believer in God. I know that me stating this may automatically irk some Christians who feel that I therefore have no right to tread as it were on their turf, territory that they hold more precious than anything else in life.

But I'm not here to argue for any theological or logical position. This may in turn annoy some atheists who want to read another article that decimates claims for the existence of a divinity. Sorry to disappoint.

I am here to praise Jesus as a teacher, someone whose words can continue to inspire. Mindfulness wasn't part of his vocabulary, nor was it amongst the methods he recommended to us if we were to seek redemption. But I believe by being mindful we can learn how to live by two of his greatest groups of teachings.

"Judge not…". Well that's straight to the point, and again…
"Let he who is without sin cast the first stone."
Even more forcefully…
"Cast out the beam of your own eye, then you'll be better able to take out the speck in your brother's eye."

For me, that's an instruction to become self-aware, to notice each and every thought and reaction that is produced by your mind. From there we can see how judgemental and critical we are of others. With this mindfulness, we let drop these judgemental views. If we do this we don't hurt others' unnecessarily, and in the next moment we may act to skilfully help the other person.

It also instructs us to focus only on our own internal flaws, not those of others. Most of the time we do the exact opposite. We notice everything wrong with others while being unable to spot our own faults and unpleasant states of mind. Don't call this hypocrisy, as that itself is just another judgement. It's simply the way the automatic mind works, but with mindfulness we can change how we react.

A second clutch of teachings from Jesus that I think especially relevant to Christmas concerns our relationship with material wealth.

"Give away all you have and follow me." Now, there's a challenge, especially on Boxing Day when all your pressies are stacked up somewhere before you've had the time to put them all away.

Later Jesus really stuck the boot in on this subject, metaphorically speaking of course. The following is one of the most stunning phrases in world history, and the least learned as a teaching.

"It is easier for a camel to pass through the eye of a needle that for a rich man to enter the kingdom of God."

I wonder if they teach that phrase at entrepreneurship lectures, or if Scottish Enterprise have a view on this. If we take it literally, and Jesus meant it literally, then the God-believing rich are gambling eighty or so years of material enjoyment against eternity of suffering.

As a non-believer I prefer to interpret Jesus's messages on wealth from a mindfulness perspective.

Our mind is shaped by our every experience. If we focus primarily on gaining wealth, and on luxuries, our mind is inevitably starved in other areas that are not being attended to. What tends to suffer is the quality of our relationships. For most of us this means family.

A stark point can be suggested. We give lots of gifts to those we love as a glitzy but flimsy compensation for not giving them what they really want, our time and our attention.

Mindfulness nurtures clear thinking and insights into what actually matters. I think Jesus's teaching in these two areas can help us to stop judging others, to notice and let go of our own ugly thoughts, and to bring our attention repeatedly to where it is most wanted, to those we love.

Have a lovely Christmas.

You and Food

How is your relationship with food? It's almost a strange kind of question to ask. It's not the sort of thing one would ask of any other living thing on the planet, with the possible exception of our pets. Most animals just search around and eat as much as they can or need at any opportunity they get.

They don't go to the shops with a list, or ponder over which brand of cereal to buy. Only we humans bring complexity to food choices and eating. Only we deliberately and knowingly eat things we know might cause us harm in the long term. Only we overeat and feel we can't prevent ourselves from doing so. Only we under-eat or reject food that we have already eaten because we're afraid we might add fat to our body.

And yet eating in or dining out are also focal points for our most important celebrations, for friends to connect, for family to sit together, for a couple to have privacy and intimacy.

At one level it's just about fuel and repair work. Our eons-honed instincts tell us when to eat, what to eat, and how to eat. The food gets broken down and separated into parts that can be burned up to give us energy to do what we need to do in life, or into parts that we need to maintain and repair the otherwise always-decaying human body we comprise of.

There's a very interesting course that starts on 20th January in Glasgow about Mindful Eating. Search for inthemomentcentre.co.uk and click on their Courses tab for further details.

It's a rare opportunity for you to learn about your own relationship to food, how you eat, why you eat the way you do, and what mindfulness practice can do to enable us to experience more and gain more joy in the moments of preparing, sharing and eating food.

We can of course blame the outside world for all our dysfunctional relationships with food. Relentless advertising of junk food. Aisles upon aisles in our supermarkets dedicated to food that has little intrinsic nutritional value. The busy nature of our lives, seeming to leave us little time to be with our food, let alone mindfully contemplate and experience it.

But here's a reality check. None of that is going to change. So you have to be the one that changes. The Glasgow mindfulness course explores nine different forms of hunger, including each of the five senses. How does your mind respond when it sees something it loves to eat, or when it smells a favourite meal when you walk by a Chinese restaurant?

Learn to consider food and eating as part of your attempts to live more mindfully. My preferred way is not to try to analyse and find out "things" about how I eat or perceive food.

Rather I allow myself simply to notice and allow the insights gained from noticing to slip into my mind subtly and gently.

It has taken you all your life to create the habitual way to you eat and relate to food. You're unlikely to change it overnight. So just take your time, observe what it actually happening in body and mind, and see if, in time, you can move to a less forced approach to food and eating, and find a newer, freer, and more uplifting relationship.

This is a very personal topic for me. Apart from the disadvantage of growing up in Scotland surrounded by an endless array of sweets as a child, I also had a momentary jolt on the subject of food. One day, eating with my myriad brothers and sisters at home I said to my mother that I didn't like the meat she had cooked, maybe because it had garlic or something new to me at that time. My father simply said "Eat it. People die because they don't have food." His mother died of starvation. He had been the witness to this, unable to help because he too was fading away, malnourished. He was just nineteen.

Food is precious and beautiful. So is your body, and your life. Try to cultivate love and appreciation of food, and enjoy eating mindfully.

Heroes and Stoicism

I don't have many heroes. Probably less than a dozen all in. The ones that spring to mind immediately are Marie Curie (Maria Sklodowska Curie as she preferred to be called), Henry David Thoreau, Thich Nhat Hanh, Ikkyu, Irena Sendler, and Hugo Ball. Yes, it sounds like a deliberately obscure, pretentious list for the most part, but I can't help that.

One other person I'd add is Marcus Aurelius. Roman Emperor. By all accounts a good one. But nowadays he is far better remembered for his privates notes to himself about life, the universe and everything. The book, now known to us as Meditations, was originally untitled as it was never intended for publication. It reads like an ongoing unformatted dumping down of reflections, usually done after a hard day's battling in wars, or doing whatever emperors did when they weren't fighting wars. It's a brilliant read, all the more so because its content is so modest, compassionate, intelligent, spiritual yet logical. It's certainly not what we'd think Roman emperors had in their heads.

Most of all philosophically, he was a Stoic. Today, stoicism is making something of a comeback, along with everything else ancient and classical. Its usage in everyday conversational verges on the pessimistic. Something along the lines of "life is really crap, accept it, and get used to it". It's a bit better than that thankfully, as is explained in a lovely new book called

More Than Happiness by Antonia Macaro. It's subtitled Buddhist and Stoic Wisdom for a Sceptical Age, and that's what makes it really interesting, because Buddhism is also sometimes inaccurately labelled as pessimistic or nihilistic.

Both philosophies start by explaining that life gives us a lot of suffering. In our age, despite healthcare, technology, scientific understanding of nutrition, central heating and comparative wealth, we still suffer.

Seemingly we are more mentally unhealthy and unhappy than previous generations. But lest we feel sorry for ourselves think about what poor Marcus or the Buddha had to put up with. Imagine a toothache two thousand years ago. No sophisticated dental care. No anaesthetics. No headache pills. A fifty-fifty chance of your newborn dying at birth or shortly thereafter. A high chance of the mother dying giving birth. A sudden downpour or cold spell ruining your harvest, raising the chances that you'd die of hunger come winter. That is if the freezing cold didn't get you first, because you have no central heating.

That's without all the stuff we still moan about. Loss of parents, arguments with spouse or partner, fall-out with siblings, rebellious children, loneliness, illnesses and diseases. There's a lot of suffering nowadays, and there was a heap more then. So the Stoics and the Buddhists were onto something.

Specifically they were trying to find ways of still living a full, purposeful and meaning life, despite all the pain that life brings.

Antonia Macaro's book is great because it not only compares and contrasts the philosophies of these two traditions and how we can perceive them in a modern light; it also does the same for the practices they recommend. She shares these in a clear, sometimes witty light. She thankfully suggests that we needn't wander about graveyards looking at the unburied decomposing bodies as was recommended by the Buddha himself as a way of seeing our physical self in a new, less egotistical and possessive way.

I'd recommend not only the book to you, but the principle behind it. Namely, that we should look back to earlier times to see what different great minds had to say about life and how to live it, without avoiding the hardest aspects. And to compare and contrast, to view these thoughts and practices critically, putting them to the test of actual experience in your own life. We are so deeply stuck in the rut of modern existence it's hard to see life for what it actually is nowadays. Marcus didn't have television, music on Spotify; he didn't tweet as his modern counterpart Donald Trump feels he has to. They were simpler times, maybe easier to spot the core truths of existence, harder to avoid both the harsh and the awesome. Marcus and the Buddha were not simple people however. They were – and remain – amongst the greatest thinkers of all time, and surely part of practice of mindfulness is to learn from the wisest.

Grateful for Life

It was my son's birthday last week.

His birth was not straightforward. Late in labour the midwives noticed signs of distress in the baby. They consulted with a specialist and an emergency operation took place immediately. Within minutes it was done. I was standing in a large pool of my wife's blood.

Our son was immediately placed in an incubator and taken away. He was still blue.

My wife was unaware of any of this. I noticed that she had turned a deeply worrying colour. I looked at the machine she was hooked up to. Her blood pressure was terribly low.

At that time a midwife literally ran out of the room and returned with packets of plasma. My wife by this time had completely lost consciousness. She was grey.

I stood, numb. I thought. The baby might be dead. My wife might be dying.

But they didn't die. This despite the fact that, as we found out by a chance glance at a medical record on our doctor's desk some time later, our son had an APGAR score of one out of ten. The APGAR measurement system is an immediate post-natal assessment of a baby's wellbeing.

It measures skin colour, pulse rate, response to stimulation, activity, and breathing. It gives a score of zero, one or two for each criterion. Our son scored nil for all of these bar one, presumably pulse rate. The difference between a score of one or two for this criterion is whether the pulse is lower than 100 beats per minute, or higher. His was presumably lower.

They owe their lives to the skills and care of the midwives, doctors and their colleagues. To those who give blood. To all of us who pay our taxes. To the vision of those who thought of, or created a health care system that allowed this to happen. To the inventors, researchers, engineers who created all the equipment that played a part in saving both their lives. And going way back in time, to every genius who made a breakthrough in understanding or practical creation of things that enabled these people to do what they did with what they had available to save these two people's lives.

Without all these people, all those thoughts, all those insights and ideas, and the compassionate mentality that drove them, my wife would have died that day. My son would have died with her. My daughter would never have been born four years later.

I have a lot to be grateful for. And I have a lot of people to thank. And there is no way I can ever thank them enough.

We were also lucky. Right at the moment my wife and my son were walking that fine line between life and death, undoubtedly other babies were dying at birth, undoubtedly mothers were dying because of similar complications. Tragically it's probably happening still, right now, at the moment I write this, and at the moment you are reading this, because many countries do not have the health care technology or systems that will save the lives of mother and baby in the same circumstance as we found ourselves in all those years ago.

Mindfulness is the skill of pausing the relentless, mostly reactive and often negative automatic stream of thoughts, emotions, and responses in everyday life. If we are mindful virtually every one of us reading this article has a thousand people to whom we owe our lives. We can replace our moaning mind, our judgemental and harsh voice inside our head through gentle but clear attention, then by letting go of the junk that's inside us.

We can replace it with a deep, inexpressible gratitude for what we have. Feeling this emotion and staying with it for a while nurtures the state of your mind for the long term. It aids a sense of peace and calmness inside you.

We can also use gratitude as an energy of compassion and altruism that helps us work towards a world where everyone has access to what we have, to what I had at that pivotal moment in four people's lives.

Compassion and altruism are as effective drivers of social and political activism as anger, and the former nurtures your being while the latter corrodes it.

All it takes is the development of paying attention on your breath. Try it. Do it. Often.

A Mindful New Generation

There appears to be yet another generational shift going on. Ironically it's the opposite of what we normally expect. Typically the younger generation rebel against the traditional or establishment way of doing things in ways which give their parents concern and anxiety. The classic examples are the immediate post-war generations, both First and Second World Wars. After the First war came the jazz age, with flappers and cocktail parties setting the scene for the upper classes in both Britain and America. The Great Gatsby best reflects this age.

Likewise it was American culture that signified best the change that came after the troops came home after the Second war. Stars like Marlon Brando and James Dean bled into the invention of the teenage rebel, with rock and roll as its back drop and teddy boys strolling the streets of London and Glasgow, trying to look dangerous and cool.

The biggest jarring between generations however came with the Sixties, the pill, the use of illegal drugs, and an explosion of creative and divergent music which ranged from The Beatles to the Velvet Underground, Frank Zappa and Captain Beefheart. I remember my father fuming at long-haired bands on the television.

So it is with some real surprise that I've read in a series of newspapers criticism of the younger generation for their interest in veganism and the growing number who have declined to make alcohol part of their lives.

From a mindfulness perspective there are always only two factors to take into account at any given time. Is what is on your mind deluded or accurate? And is what you are about to do likely to be good for you and those around you, or potentially harmful?

With alcohol it's sadly straightforward. People drink alcohol because it has become a habit in their lives. It has become a habit because of several things; peer pressure when they were younger; a perceived impression that it makes you look cooler or part of the group; and that it is an effective and harmless way to relax. Moreover all of these things are supported by the marketing strategies of all the major manufacturers of alcoholic drinks.

However the UK government's guidelines on alcohol since 2016 states very clearly that there is no such thing as any safe limit on drinking alcohol and that any amount can increase the chances of cancer.

It's a similar story with the trend towards veganism, though the numbers are still very small, at less than 1% of the population in the UK. But almost half of all vegans are under the age of 35. Their reason is simple; ethics. They believe that meat and dairy products require the killing and suffering of all the animals in the process, and that this can be avoided by eating only plant-based products. The same applies to animal-based non-foodstuffs such as leather belts and bags and much more.

So the generation currently in their teens, twenties or early thirties seem to be rebelling against what they deem to be the sins of their parents. But the senior generation have been programmed into their way of living, through cultural and big business conditioning, so it's not their fault. Moreover there is certainly within our gene pool the desire and capacity to ear meat, and to seek chemicals that alter our state of mind. This latter characteristic appears to be in almost all cultures going well back into the earliest records of tribes around the world.

What, from a mindfulness perspective, is especially gratifying is that this upcoming generation have chosen their own health, and the welfare of other living things in their choices of lifestyle. With the concurrent growth of mindfulness in people of all ages we can perceive a pattern of people wanting to be in control of who they are, trying to assess what is good about traditions and what is harmful or useless, and trying to avoid the latter.

I think this is very different from the staid, puritanical approach that dominated the Scottish establishment for centuries before the post-war baby boom. That was based on a harsh interpretation of Christianity that emphasised sin, punishment and joylessness. What our young people are choosing now is to not cause harm to anything and anyone, but to seek joy and happiness in safer, simpler ways. Surely that is to be welcomed.

Mindfulness is for Life

We have grown impatient as a species, or at least amongst those of us who live in the most economically developed parts of the world. With relentless industrialisation and technological innovation we have come to expect solutions at the click of a finger, or rather, the press of a button on our smart phone.

If the internet is slow we feel irritated and frustrated. We search for replies to our emails and messages on social media within minutes of sending them. Our managers at work expect instant answers, day or night in some cases.

But some things simply don't come quickly. No matter how quickly you would like your baby to walk, it has to go through a growing and developing process. It's the same with the development of speech in an infant. Given due love and attention, encouragement and playful coaxing, the skills of walking and talking usually emerge over time.

In a similar way we develop all sorts of traits. They take time to develop, some more than others. Lifelong genetic traits such as bad-temperedness or kindness can be seen in toddlers, but other traits develop more as a result of familial, local or national culture and individual life experiences. These emerge over time in a complex, ever-shifting ebb and flow of life events and responses.

It is usually impossible to point exactly to what combination of experiences and genetic tendencies lead to certain challenging states of mind, such as depression, anxiety, anger or chronic stress. There's a tendency or temptation to point to a single major event and assume it's the sole cause of a particular state of mind. But the reality is usually far more complex, comprising of a vast amount of experiences and inherent tendencies coming together to result in a negative prolonged mental state. The same is true for positive states of mind, though ironically these are far less researched and understood, such is our fascination with negativity.

Sometimes single events do result instantly in a massive change of mood or view. This has been reported in both positive and negative cases, but they are by far the exception. Normally particular long-lasting states of mind and traits take years or even decades to develop.

Mindfulness helps us work on these states of mind or traits. However, just as they usually take decades to develop, so the process of unwinding or unlearning these can take similar lengths of time. We need to be patient with our mindfulness practice. It is not something that works overnight, although it often provides some short-term longed-for relief from the worst aspects of our negative mental states.

Ironically patience itself is a highly-skilled mental trait. Some people seem to have it from birth, others are not so fortunate.

So a skill we need in order to stick with mindfulness is often not inherently in some people. Unless they get instant relief or change they lose patience with the practice and give it up.

What usually happens with such people is that a few days or weeks later they realise that they have no Plan B to deal with their negativity, so go back to trying mindfulness. Again the lack of immediate results kicks off another bout of impatience, and the unhelpful cycle recommences. We can only hope in these circumstances that enough of the skill of mindfulness sticks that at some point it wins against the impatience long enough for the individual to build a new routine of mindful practice in their life. I have seen this happen, so it's not all bad news for those of you who are inherently impatience.

The same is true for the deeply sceptical and the cynical amongst us. Borderline dismissive right from the start, unless it helps straight away, such people reject the practices as a con. The irony is that this type of person probably needs mindfulness more than most of us, as their blinkered, closed-minded life view means they experience less of the joys of life than is out there.

Mindfulness is a lifelong practice. I've been doing it for twenty years, benefitted immensely from it through those two decades, and I intend to continue to use it to ward off my worst personal traits and nurture my best qualities for the rest of my life. I hope you will too.

Politicians and Bosses Need Mindfulness

Who we are and how we view the world is not as it seems. We tend to think that we work at developing our best traits while controlling our worst, and at the same time we rationally absorb the news and slowly develop a clear logical political, social and economic viewpoint.

That's not what science tells us. It tells us that we are born with innate personality tendencies and that these are constantly moulded and shaped through our lives, for the most part without us being aware that it's happening, and not only in our early years but all through our lifetime. Moreover a series of studies indicate that specific genes influence our political views, to roughly the same extent as they shape our personality. A U.S. study suggests that political conservative views are 64.5 percent heritable in men, and 44.7 percent in women.

We then reinforce these. If we have strong inherent views we tend to read and watch media that confirm rather than challenge our views, so most people unconsciously nurture their genetic political perspectives, while thinking that they are reasoning their way through what are invariably complex issues.

Our civil servants any politicians, right up to the First Minister, Prime Minister, and President of the European Council are no exceptions to this natural tendency.

Thus, unless they have consciously and assiduously worked to rebalance their unconscious and unreasoned political biases, they carry them with them in every arena of their work.

The same is true for bosses in businesses and other organisations.

I believe that more than anything else a leader should have a clear, calm mind. This makes them able to resist knee-jerk reactions, avoid angry and spiteful responses, and take into consideration the whole picture rather than a narrow, blinkered view. This doesn't mean that if our politicians, business leaders and other influential people deliberately and rigorously cultivated their best qualities of mind, they'd all reach agreement on every matter. Most issues are not simple, with gaps in the knowledge needed to be certain about the way ahead, and there's always the unknowability of future events that may scupper the best laid plans. However it would mean that their genetic and life-skewed political and personal biases would play a lesser part in decision-making.

Linked to this is the second most important quality I think a leader should have, which is a combination of kindness, empathy, and compassion. If our leaders could cultivate clarity and calmness, manage and reduce their innate biases, while genuinely feeling deep in their heart that they want what is best for all – and that may include animals and the environment – I think most people would agree that the quality of such leadership would be first-rate.

It would be very interesting to know to what extent if at all, our politicians and government officials have been trained in mindfulness as a means of improving their decision-making, for the benefit of all they are there to serve. And if trained in mindfulness, how many make the time to practice regularly so that it can have a positive effect on their abilities. Or do they rely on what's already controlling and influencing their minds as things stand at present, oblivious to unconscious bias which may include gender inequality, exploitation of power, manipulation, unpleasantness, egotism rather than the greater good, and so many other traits from those in power that we see from time to time on the front pages of our newspapers?

Every one of us is in a position of power. It's not just the politicians and business people. The person who most influences your life moment by moment is you. Will you grimace or will you smile? Will you buckle under pressure or know how to let it go and thus avoid harmful consequences? Will you cross the street or give a homeless person some money? Can you take a deep breath and go to your boss and them that something wrong and unfair is happening in the organisation?

We all have our own sphere of influence, starting with ourselves. So keep practising your mindfulness, moment by moment when you can, and if the politicians and business leaders do so as well we might just find ourselves slowly moving into an era of healthier and fairer times.

Rethinking our Purpose

The forecasts are alarming, and probably alarmist but the suggestion that automation, robot workers, and driverless vehicles will wipe out large sections of employment worldwide is something we need to be thinking about.

Some of us have witnessed this kind of story before. In the early to mid-seventies books were published forecasting a new golden age of leisure, because productivity due to computer-based technology would give us the twin blessing of economic growth and shorter working hours. We'd all be working ten hours a week on full pay.

How wrong that was. Two generations of some desperately unfortunate families have been squeezed out of employment by rising expectations of what a satisfactory employee must show. Large numbers are working on zero hours or part-time contracts when many of these workers would prefer the greater job security, pay, and stability of a permanent full-time job. Ironically however, rather than a golden age of leisure we have a harsher age of overwork and stress-inducing jobs.

So we should take with a pinch of salt the claims that automation will wipe us all out of work, though it is always hard to predict the future so it just might happen. Time will tell.

What it does stimulate us to do is to consider the big question of purpose. What are you for? Some predict that even top professional jobs will be taken by artificially intelligent machines that think smarter, faster, and crucially, cheaper than you. There are already machines that can create good art and fine poetry, and we're just at the beginning of this journey into the unknown.

So who are you if not your job title? If not a circle of community with your colleagues?

Imagine for a second the good version of this scenario comes to pass, whereby automation brings fantastic global wealth which is then shared fairly so that all us ex-employees and bosses have a lifetime's income sufficient to lead a pretty decent, if not extravagant life.

There would still be fifteen or sixteen waking hours to fill every day. There's no voluntary work because the robots have taken all those too. The housework can get done by them, and the meals cooked by them after they've delivered the shopping for you.

What are you left with if you have nothing to do? What is the core purpose of existence once the essentials have been secured? Can you just be? Can you be fulfilled just being part of nature, but without other animals' needs to find food, build shelter, seek clean water? It's the classic science-fiction scenario of a species with no purpose.

This gets to the heart, maybe the mystery, of what it is to be human. As a result of pure chance we were born in this time with all the riches and problems of our age. We are also the product not only of our parents' genes but of the culture, technology, morality and rituals of our time. We have more than any other generation of humanity. More material products. More labour-saving devices. More forms of entertainment. More access to knowledge. More knowledge. More fake news. More opportunity to see the world.

Most of this we use primarily to fill the time or to satisfy our addiction to novelty and surprise. Is this what we will do even more of? A vacuous never-ending line of entertainment, like a type of white line of cocaine laid out upon the table of our lives, to be sniffed endlessly, so that we're forever on an entertainment or fun high? That's what the film Wall-E portrayed.

In my view we're already half-way there, in a confusion of too much, whilst not having a clue about where we are going as a species or what we are to do on this Earth with the limited time available to us, that period we call life. So we get caught up in petty squabbles over power or rule; we call these wars or politics or constitutional crises. Meanwhile the substance of our lives, moments, those precious blips of time during which we can experience what it actually means or feels to be alive, those priceless gems slip through our fingers as if they were part of an infinite source of sand. But they are not infinite. The sands of time run dry, and then you've had it. No more moments.

Make time to think on what matters in life, and what doesn't. Learn to know the difference and learn to appreciate your precious one chance at life.

Judgement-Free Justice

One of the most fascinating and challenging aspects in recent neuroscientific research is the question of the extent to which we can actually control ourselves. In particular a few separately conducted studies show that we – ie. our brains - make their mind up about a choice even while we think we're still deciding. Using MRI scanners the researchers have been able to show with uncanny accuracy what people have decided even before they think they have actually decided.

Are we automatons, doomed to live according to the unconscious workings of our mind? Looks like it is.

Even if it's not yet proven, it is interesting to cast a mindful eye on what the implications might be if this were the case, and how we all might feel more relaxed and less bitter if we viewed each other as just either lucky or unlucky in the mind stakes. If someone does us wrong, we simply let it go. Why? Because we accept that they were hardwired to act like that, and if we were them we'd have done the same thing, because that's how their brain worked at that time.

No more blame.

In place of hatred and bitterness, sadness and compassion for the poor soul condemned to make such terrible decisions.

In place of judgement, condemnation, haughty words from the judges, a criminal is sent to a humane secure place so that he or she might be kept away from people she might harm, but is not thought of as evil. Just badly wired by genes and life experiences.

If we viewed everyone through such a lens we might perform better the rehabilitation functions of the justice system, something that we do see progressing in our time, but the task is long and arduous. Minds moulded to react with anger or cruelty are not readily or easily reshaped into socially acceptable reactions and thoughts. Guilt, bitterness, resentment, and denial only hinder the mental work that needs to be done if we are to help people change long-standing conditioning.

However it is not just those whose minds create impulses to harm or mock or exploit who might benefit from a different take on how the mind works. We too, assuming you the reader are an upstanding individual, can have a much happier life as a result.

Imagine not having relentless judgemental thoughts or criticisms of people. Imagine we as a society no longer had people writing messages such as "scum", "castrate the bastard" and other similar raging responses on social media whenever someone is found guilty, or even just accused of some of the worst forms of sexual or violent crime.

None of this is to be soft on crime. I am absolutely clear that if someone poses a danger to the public they should be kept in a secure place, and if that individual cannot or will not change, and be proven to have changed, then we need to keep him or her securely away from the public, even if that means till death.

Rather it is about our culture, our mental culture. In my mindful opinion it harms not only the perpetrator, but the victim's family and friends, and the general public. Changing our mindset on how we understand the root causes and the absence of real choice in some people's minds can free us of emotions and reactions that we know harm our own health.

Moreover, such a radically different perspective on how we all make decisions and do what we do, can help create a new culture in Scotland, where respect and compassion replace condemnation and hatred. It may also nurture in us as a society a stronger sense of positive creativity, focussed solely on making constructive change rather than on punitive reactions to past events.

We should be science-led in our thinking and our decision-making, and we should be warm-hearted especially when the science encourages us to be so. The great beauty of this, the mindful approach to living, is that it not only results in greater calmness and kindness, but in being much more productive and results-orientated because our minds are no longer cluttered with distracting negative judgements all the time.

So get your mindfulness cap on, look up the science on the mind's decision-making processes, do the mindfulness practices available via Google and You Tube or my own site, and start to deprogramme your judgemental mind.

Social Engineering the Mindfulness Way

Every so often one group of political activists or a spokesperson accuse the other side of social engineering when a new policy is introduced. More often it is the right criticising the left because of the left's tendency to have state intervention as a strategy to try to change social injustices or help the weakest and most vulnerable. Sometime though the charge has been made in the opposite direction, where the left criticise the right for trying to engineer a selfish, individualist culture where all that matters is entrepreneurship and money-making, and the cultivation of people who can do this.

Ironically what neither side notices is that social engineering is part of what we are as a species. We are inherently and continually socially-engineered. You, reading this, are being socially engineered by my words. The engineering might be to agree with my points and possibly reinforce some views you already had. Or you might vehemently disagree with what I say, and thus be engineered in a different direction.

In neuroscience terms social engineering is called neuroplasticity, the constant effect of experiences on the brain, our personality and traits.

So the question is not, should we try to socially engineer people but rather, who should be doing the engineering, and in what direction should this shaping of people go?

Libertarians argue that the best thing is to leave it to chance. Minimise state interference, and all will balance out for the greater good. It's interesting though that they believe in laws to protect property and assets, laws which themselves surely cause social engineering of the highest order.

Socialists tend to go in the opposite direction and try to deliberately engineer. A classic example was Tony Blair's "early intervention" policies designed to give very young children opportunities to those who may otherwise not have been given the benefits of education and love of learning at home.

Religion used to be the most dominant form of social engineering. By the age of four I was taught the first pages of the Catechism, words which are embedded in my mind:

Who made me?

God made me.

Why did God make me?

God made me to know Him, to love Him, and to serve Him so that I may be happy with Him forever in Heaven.

This is powerful. In two sentences, before I finished first year at primary school I knew a version of how I was made, a whole life purpose, and a reason for having that life purpose.

I also had no doubt from this programming that God was male. I don't use the word "programmed" as a negative, simply to describe how such teachings enter the brain and influence a person's life.

The fact that this remains so deeply ingrained in my mind suggests the extent of its influence on me. No doubt in other families, different beliefs or philosophies will have been programmed into the heads of children.

We are programmed by our family, often unconsciously and therefore unintentional. Growing up in Scotland in the 1960s I somehow became programmed to dislike something called "the English" or "England", meaning mostly the English football team, but sometimes more broadly. Sadly many were programmed in religious prejudice between Catholics and Protestants. These are examples of socially engineering through programming.

Mindfulness applied and taught to others is a fascinating form of social engineering, as one of its key benefits is to nurture a clear, calm mind that, amongst other things, comes to notice the prejudices and programmes already deep inside us. So at its heart it is a form of social engineering that enables us to de-engineer ourselves, and should we wish, to re-engineer in a direction which we, now as freer individuals, choose for ourselves, to the extent that any human can.

Look at your reactions to things. What do you instantly dislike? What do you instantly support? Can you calmly assess how that view came to be in your mind?

Can you then more clearly assess its positive or negative influence on you and those around you? If negative can you let it go just this one time? If so, you have started to socially-re-engineer yourself, this time by yourself, for yourself.

A Mindful Nation

It starts with just one person. You perhaps. Dedicating a small part of your day every day to nurture your peace of mind, and clear away all the irks and accumulated baggage of the past. In time your mind become clearer, so you make wiser decisions, refrain from knee-jerk reactions, and everyone around you benefits from your clarity of thought.

In time your mind becomes calmer, more tranquil, so you let things go that you previously might have reacted negatively to. Because of this you stop collecting baggage, and a lot of the old resentments, prejudices and irrational dislikes that you've gathered over decades, start to dissipate from the core of your mind.

You become increasingly liberated, freed from the junk of life, and in that new clear space you can flourish with an open mind, and a wish to do no harm to anything that lives, and to help where you can. It doesn't matter whether you're the First Minister, a nurse, the CEO of a major FTSE global corporation, or an unemployed man or woman. Your mind is quite simply better than it was before, and not only you, but all those around you will benefit from the change inside you.

If we can spread it from just one person, to two, to twenty two, to two thousand, to two hundred thousand, to two million, finally to all 5.5 million of us here in Scotland, think what that would mean to us all.

The prisons emptied. No more bigotry. No more racism. No more sexism. Rational, open-minded political and constitutional discussions. A more prosperous economy because our business people have sharper minds, but a fairer one because everyone realises we all need all of us on board and sharing what we gain.

I know. Some of you might be thinking this is La La Land. Maybe it is. But each and every step in that direction makes someone's life better, and that is not an unrealistic dream. And if you can transform one person's life then, all else being equal, you can do the same for five million people, over time, with a clear vision, a sound strategy, and properly budgeted.

I have personally witnessed people emerge from degrees of anxiety so bad that they fear leaving their home, people who moved from being suicidal to regaining a love of life. I have answered questions on the mind and the challenge of changing what's inside them, from prisoners in Scotland's highest security prisons, prisoners who want to totally change but need the tools and the motivation. Change is possible. The research does show this. The extent to which such change can be achieved depends on the unique make up of each person. Maybe some people can't change their genetic or life-shaped destructive or unhappy mental traits, but we don't know that, so we should work on the assumption that people can change, and help them try to do so if they want it.

There are concerns about such a vision, and about using mindfulness to achieve it. Many centre around a profound misunderstanding of what mindfulness is, namely the idea of a fluffy, new age, stress relief thing. The other concern relates to how a philosophy and set of practices like mindfulness fit or don't fit with existing faiths add philosophies, especially as mindfulness was in fact created as a method by the Buddha. But in my experience mindfulness can sit perfectly comfortably with all faiths and with agnostics and atheists, and indeed can enhance their own understanding of their way of seeing life, because the clarity of thought that mindfulness brings may bring new insights into faiths and philosophies, to the benefit of the individual.

So let's not do this mindfulness thing quietly and meekly. Why not imagine a completely mentally healthy Scottish population, from babies to folk celebrating their one hundredth birthday? I really believe, if we actually want it deep down, that we can reduce and ultimately eliminate all of the mental traits that so inhibit of love of life. I believe we can use mindfulness to so improve our thinking abilities and our sense of altruism and compassion, that these qualities combined can help us help those who have suffered most in our society, and those whose destructive or self-destructive behaviours stem from neglected or violent upbringings.

But first of all we need to work on ourselves, and we need a clear vision of a healthy, peaceful Scotland. Let's go for it.

Truth Versus What Works

My mother died less than four weeks after the death of my father. A few days after his funeral she fell into something like a coma, from which she awoke from time to time. She had already been diagnosed with a terminal form of cancer. It was agreed amongst the family and with the medical experts caring for her that she should be allowed home to die.

However both my parents seemed to have acquired super-human genes so instead of what we all thought, that she would pass away within a day or two of her coming home, she instead clung on for another ten days. She had round the clock care, and as we are a large family, she had several of us with her at all times for the remaining days of her life.

My mother was born and raised a Catholic, and stayed true to that faith right until she died. I don't share that faith, though it's how I was raised as a child. I have no religious affiliation and try to remain respectful towards all people's beliefs. What strikes me with regard to my mother's faith was how much it sustained her through her whole life, including my father's death and her own painful and grief-filled last few weeks. When we were with her in those last days she asked us to pray, even though she knew many of us had no religion. My daughter decided to learn the prayers by heart so she could say them, to please her dying grandmother.

My mother wasn't asking us to say prayers for her; it was for us. Despite bring hurt that many of us had abandoned the faith that she so strongly adhered to, she felt that our lack of belief might cause us to be punished by God after we died, as her faith teaches. So in her death bed, for days on end, she tried to help us save our souls.

It's a testimony of her love for us, and the final scenes based on a faith that she trusted and which she leant on through her entire life. This leads me to a personal view, that what works can be more effective even if it's not proven to be true.

At this point those of you reading who are Catholic mighty say it just proves that my mother's faith reflected the Truth and that such faith shows that God is merciful, just and kind. However the same support, resilience and benefits have been experienced by Muslims, Hindus, Buddhists, Jews and those of other faiths, and by atheists. Given that each of these have different beliefs, the benefits they bring to believers can't all be put down to the fact that theirs is the real truth.

I believe it is the combination of deep conviction about something on the one hand, and the power of the human mind to create and imagine a belief to be real, that creates this powerful effect. So we can benefit from beliefs, even if imagined, even if not the Truth.

Consider the placebo effect. A pill whose chemical makeup provides no benefits in itself, does provide benefits if the person believes it will. Even more remarkably taking a pill knowing that it is just a placebo still provides benefits simply because we associate taking pills with giving positive results. What's happening is that the brain responds to perceived thoughts even if they're not true.

I use words frequently through the day to ease or change my mindset. When I'm tired I can just think "rest" or "peace" or "relax", usually in conjunction with my breath, because the breath itself is an inherently easy, pleasant, soft thing to notice.

So we can imagine our reality, our mood, our reaction to events. This can be a helpful tool to soothe our stressful mind, and to give us strength when we feel tired, afraid or anxious.

Knowing that this is proven, we can use our mindfulness to bring these remarkable tools to bear whenever we feel negative in our life. In other words if your life doesn't feel right at any time, recreate it with strong belief and imagination, moment by moment by moment.

The Long View and the Present Moment

The skill of mindfulness is the practice of noticing what's going on, externally and internally, moment by moment through your day. What many people think of when they hear the word "mindfulness" is not this. They think of it as the practice, often called mindfulness meditation, but this in fact is simply the way we train the mind to become better at being mindful in everyday life. Think of it as similar to going for a run. The point of going for a run is to maintain and develop fitness, and we want to be fit in order to do more in our lives and to live longer.

It's the same with mindfulness. We do the training bit regularly not for its own sake, but in order to be more aware, more mindful, in everyday life, and thus be more likely not to think, communicate or act unhelpfully, and be more likely to enjoy and contribute to whatever is happening in our lives.

However what do we mean by the present moment, and what does it all imply about us thinking about the future and reflecting on ongoing matter such as political or social issues?

The present moment is a fleeting and strange thing. As soon as you try to notice it, it's gone, to be replaced by another one, but then it's gone too. But this is to try to notice the moment as a concept, as something we can define.

Being aware of what's happening in the present however, is not a concept, it's not abstract. It's real, often raw, immediate, and very powerful if we give it full attention.

Here's an example from a couple of minutes ago. I put out my bin for collection. It was on one of those days where the bcast from the east returned briefly. Because I was only taking the bin a matter of a few meters I didn't put any winter clothing on top of my gym top and trousers. It was minus two degrees and felt like minute nine. But the early morning sun was shining on me. The experience therefore was acute; exceptionally bitter on my fingers and hands, on my cheeks, and through my top onto my chest and body. But because I was only outside for less than a minute these felt more sharp than unpleasant, a sense of extreme but not painful sensation of touch. Moreover the sun was remarkably bright, bringing crispness, light, and deep shade to the scene, which was one of a dusting of snow but many areas uncovered. My eyes saw all this and my brain translated it into a sense of beauty, almost awe. Put together I experienced a sense of joy of being alive… while putting the bin out. How cool is that?

Earlier, on the morning news, the story was still all about the attempted murder of the Russian ex-spy and his daughter, the death of a second Russian man, and the political fall out between Downing Street and the Kremlin. The news reader was speaking in the present, about a series of episodes from the fairly recent past. She discussed the possible consequences with another reporter.

This therefore was conjecture about the future. Watching this without mindfulness I would have been mentally dragged into the past to a place and to people I didn't know, then into an as-yet experienced future, with all sorts of options, none of which were presented as positive, but rather, things to be concerned about.

Meanwhile I was sitting absorbing this in a living room in Hamilton. It will come as no surprise to you that I don't have Vladimir Putin or Teresa May's phone numbers, so couldn't give them a ring to ask questions about the truth of these sad matters, nor offer any advice, if asked, about the best way to resolve the matters for the good of the world. Frankly I can't think of any way I can help the situation. I mindfully noticed that this was the case and switched off the television. That's when I put out the bin. I had changed my life activities from a useless, potentially harmful one, namely worrying about the world situation when I couldn't contribute usefully to it, to a positive action, doing a household task that needed to be done.

In the grand scheme of things it was no great mindful decision, but given the options I had in those particular moments, I made a better, and declined a lesser decision.

Hope you have a lovely day, filled with mindful moments of enjoyment, kindness and pleasure.

The Beatles on Mindfulness

"When I find myself in times of trouble mother Mary comes to me, speaking words of wisdom, 'Let it be'"

All four of the Beatles had more than their fair share of troubles, much of which comes with the pressures of fame and the machinations of business when it comes into contact with the arts and creativity. At one level they were four ordinary working class guys from Liverpool, but simultaneously and paradoxically, they were unique and ingenious as individuals and as a close group of friends.

How they handled the unprecedented challenges that came with their mind-boggling level of success as young men is laid out both consciously and unconsciously in the lyrics of many of their songs. I think they can be used by all of us as reminders to practice mindfulness on the one hand, and to benefit from listening to the beauty and insight of their songs. We can listen mindfully, with effortless but clear attention, so that it seems we are hearing the tune, the harmonies and the words for the first time.

Let's start with clear thinking. Paul McCartney's words again. "Life is very short and there's no time for fussing and fighting my friend… We can work it out". In this beautiful song there's not just insight and clarity, but a sense of what matters in life, and a compassionate view of the other person.

You can almost hear McCartney having the conversation with the other person, and the fear of the other being hurt by mindless knee-jerk reactions.

George Harrison wrote some of the most spiritual and deeply introspective songs of any music artist of our time. In the song "I Me Mine" on their last album "Let it Be" he sings mournfully about the band falling out and becoming self-serving. "All I can hear, I me mine I me mine I me mine". As with McCartney you can hear the combination of loss and wishing it were otherwise.

Poets and other artists often have great mindful insights without even being aware that they are doing so. But all four members of The Beatles studied eastern philosophies and mindfulness, and consciously put what they learned from these experiences into their later songs.

John Lennon's classic Strawberry Fields Forever is a case in point. At first listening it may sound like a nonsense, drug-influenced song. "Nothing is real and nothing to get hung about". But this is in fact one of the great insights of mindfulness and modern science alike. What we think is real is only our mind's interpretation or reworking of sensory input. This is especially important to understand regarding our emotional reactions to events. The mind creates feelings of depression, sadness, worry, anxiety and we automatically think what it's telling us about life a situation is real. Often it's not. Usually our automatic reaction sees the worst-case scenario, and a few moments of quiet observation can lead us to a much more positive and helpful response.

Lennon becomes even more explicit and insightful. "Living is easy with eyes closed, misunderstanding all you see." This is precisely what mindfulness teaches us from observing moment by moment experiences of our mind and the outside world. We are blinkered, "eyes closed". We don't see the full picture, only what our closed eyes, our automatic reactions, tell us. And what does it tells us? It causes us to misunderstand all we see.

This is the cause of most of our woes in life, a blinkered, misunderstood series of responses to events in life. It's also the cause of all the world's political woes. This inability to see what is real is tragic and devastating to many.

On a totally different front, but just as important, if not as profound, is Ringo Starr's late response to the tensions and struggles of the final period of the Beatles as band. Always dismissed as the least creative, and self-deprecating by nature, Ringo still had some beautiful moments of insight and emotional intelligence.

The song "Octopus's Garden" is, like the most famous song he sang, "Yellow Submarine" often considered a song for children, but consider the lyrics from a point of view of four close friends falling apart.
"I'd like to be under the sea in an octopus's garden in the shade... I'd ask my friends to come and see... we would be warm below the storm in our little hideaway beneath the waves... we would sing and dance around because we know we can't be found."

How poignant is this? How eloquent an expression of wanting to escape pain and pressures, and try to find a space where dear friends could recuperate and perhaps recover their true relationships?

Back to McCartney again. "And in the end the love you take is equal to the love you make".

There is magic in music and wisdom in lyrics. Try to understand afresh, in a different, mindful way, what messages may arise in your mind from listening to the old songs you know and love. Mindful listening can transform your mind and make it come alive again.

As the Beatles sang in the exquisite song Blackbird "All your life you were only waiting for this moment to be free". Make the most of your moments.

They are all you have.

Freedom of Speech and Mindfulness

The pen is mightier than the sword, so the saying goes. But hit someone with a sword, and belittle someone with words, and the criminal justice system historically will view the former as criminal and the latter as nothing to do with them.

Another old phrase is "Sticks and stones make break my bones, but names will never hurt me." Try telling that to the families of people who killed themselves after receiving vindictive or unpleasant abuse over social media or face to face.

We currently have what I consider a much-needed and major debate about the principle of freedom of speech and limitations on this freedom. Freedom of speech is an iconic and much-loved human right. Yet here in Scotland and in the rest of the UK we have what are commonly referred to as hate crimes, which are essentially thoughts put into words. So we have thought crimes (as soon as the thoughts are translated into words).

This spills into politics and history. Sixteen European countries and Israel have introduced legislation criminalising denial of the Holocaust. The UK and USA have not. Earlier this year Poland made it a crime to state that the Polish Nation or government participated in or supported the Holocaust in German-occupied Poland. This caused an outcry across the world.

People who are put on trial, even when found not guilty suffer the automatic reaction of much of public opinion, including large sections of the media, which, contrary to the maxim, innocent until proven guilty, conclude that someone is guilty if arrested. These individuals suffer enormous stress, humiliation and depression even after the verdict of not guilty is pronounced.

The same abuse, pain and bewilderment often faces those who claimed to be victims of a crime, if the result of the case is a not guilty verdict. People, usually through social media, heap verbal abuse on these individuals, automatically assuming they made up the story, rather than the alternative possibility, namely that the jury simply didn't have enough evidence to convict. This causes most anguish and difficulty when it happens in rape trials.

We are clearly in a world where how and what we communicate has become a much more free-wheeling and challenging thing to understand and respond to in a sane, wise way. Yet sound advice exists. Around 500 BC two great thinkers looked at this problem before any form of communication other than speech was in common usage.

Gautama Siddhartha, the Buddha, devoted one of his eight "paths" to freedom to this subject. He called it Right Speech, with the word Right meaning speech that aims to achieve constructive or helpful outcomes. Look at any political or news comments and see how few meet that noble purpose.

He explained his definition of Right Speech, as explained by Walpola Sri Rahula in the classic "What the Buddha Taught" which I recommend wholeheartedly. Right speech is "friendly and benevolent, pleasant and gentle, meaningful and useful". He goes on to say that "if one cannot say something useful, one should keep a noble silence". How many times have we wished that other people did just that? How many times would it have been better if we had just refrained from reacting with harsh and unwarranted words?

The other great teacher of that time was the author or authors of the book in verse, the Tao te Ching, commonly attributed to Lao Tzu. In the last of its eighty-one verses the poet says "Good people do not quarrel. Quarrelsome people are not good."

In an earlier passage it says "those who would be above must speak as if they are below. Those who would lead must speak as if they are behind." In other words be humble and considerate in your speech, not arrogant and reactive as if your every word should be heeded.

Despite developing our skill in constructive communication we still may differ from one another about the pros and cons of legislation on communication. Being mindful does not mean everyone reaches agreement on all matters. But I think we must should educate not just the school age generation, but all generations, about skilful and constructive communicating, and the consequences of destructive and hurtful words.

Something does not have to be illegal to make it wrong, and something does not have to be physical to cause great harm, even loss of life. As the great Dylan Thomas put it in one of his rare political poems "The hand that signed a paper felled a city." Through regular practice of mindfulness methods we develop skill in constructive and productive communication, so that we never have to think "these fingers that typed a comment harmed a life" or damaged a mind.

The opposite effect is possible. The words we use can lift someone out of their own embedded hateful thought. Your words can nurture a person's understanding of how to live life more fully and enjoyably. Your words can put a smile on someone's face, or at the very least, bring a little ray of light or hope, to someone who is desolate. These results of your own fully developed right speech are achievable, not just occasionally but every single day, and in this way you play your part in detoxifying the world of communications, and replacing it with thoughtful, kind tones.

Trust and Society

Trust is a vital part of any relationship. This is true whether we're talking about a close, intimate relationship, or in the workplace, and indeed in society as a whole. Many decades ago, during a discussion in our family business my eldest brother told me of something he had read about trust. It suggested that rust had three separate aspects. Honesty, competence, and reliability.

Let's leave Honesty aside for the moment as I'll focus on that for the rest of this article. We can briefly look at each of the other two aspects.

George Best was far more than competent at football. He was a genius. However he was not reliable. His managers couldn't predict whether he'd play well or not in any particular game, and as his life grew more chaotic, they couldn't rely on him turning up for training, occasionally even for matches.

At a much more mundane level, I once had an employee who was utterly reliable, but as technology came into the areas of her work she balked at learning the new way we had to do things, and refused to commit to learning. She became increasingly incompetent at the job she was doing, so we couldn't trust her to do it to the standards needed. We had to move her to a different role.

We need to have confidence in the people we depend on to do what they do to a certain standard, and we need to be able to rely on them to actually do what they said they'd do.

That said flaws such as incompetence and unreliability can usually be put down to personal traits or characteristics and we can all agree that no one is perfect.

However when it comes down to honesty we see things from a much more judgemental position. If someone deliberately cheats on us or steals or is in some other way dishonest, we perceive that as of an altogether higher category of untrustworthiness than incompetence and unreliability.

Practising mindfulness helps us to notice things more clearly and calmly, with a compassionate mind. When we observe the behaviour and attitude of leaders with this mindful attention we start to be aware of a series of societally-destructive consequences when honesty is lacking. Precisely because of the exalted position of leadership the results of their dishonesty cascade down from the top, sometimes to an entire population.

Recent news has been full of accusations of corruption by political leaders and ex-leaders. Brazil's Lula, Sarkozy of France, Netanyahu in Israel, South Korea's Park Geun-hye, and Zuma in South Africa. Each of these has either been convicted, is on trial right now or is facing investigation.

Donald Trump is under investigation regarding potentially criminal activities during his election campaign, while the Russian leader, Putin has faced multiple accusations over the years.

This does not prove the rule that power corrupts but the result of the sheer scale of these accusations over the years is that our trust in leadership generally has been eroded.

Other pillars of society which at one time were considered trustworthy have crumbled. Whether it is covering up child abuse in religious denominations, media intrusion on ordinary people's privacy, deliberate hacking or production of fake news by national governments and media, constant attempts by big business to bribe national governments or mislead the consumer, key structures of societies have lost much of our trust in them.

Where there is little trust people become cynical, apathetic or more extremist. At an unconscious level people reason that if they can't trust their own religion, their elected politicians, the media through which they keep abreast of events, and the businesses from which they buy life's essentials, then they change how they perceive society as a whole, and accordingly how they live their lives.

Some bow out, believing that everyone and everything is corrupt, that there's little left we can trust. This is despair often disguised as cynicism. As such it is a deeply unhealthy and self-harming state of mind.

Others get stressed, anxious and depressed as a direct result of having few or no societal pillars on which to rely. This too is mentally destructive.

A small number reject the entire way we have structured our society and seek a violent solution in order to bring back what they believe to have been a previous age of honesty and stability. The hatred and prejudice towards others that this brings is not only socially troubling but develops poorer mental health in the individual.

This situation present us with two simultaneous challenges. As a society we need to raise the levels of trustworthiness in our key institutions and their leaders. This is no easy task, especially in politics where the pressure on leaders to please the public and be media-obsessed is itself corrupting. But we need to work on it mindfully and strategically. Trust should not be left to chance.

The other challenge is for all of us to build resilience in the face of the absence of societal trust. Just because some leaders and institutions seem to be untrustworthy does not mean that all are. Moreover just because some elements of society are exploitative and corrupt does not mean that all aspects of our daily lives are devoid of joy and beauty.

For both, the leaders and ourselves, a mind that sees clearly and realistically, compassionately and calmly, can help change this troubling aspect of our society.
Mindfulness practices can help as a long-term and constructive way of getting us out of this situation. Practice, practice, practice.

Rain – A Reflection

When I thought of the word "rain" three things came to mind, reflecting deeply ingrained stuff in my mind.

The short story of that name by William Somerset Maugham. It's a grim, claustrophobic story, one of the best short stories written according to those who decide these things. Set in the Pacific island of American Samoa during days of incessant tropical rainstorms, it examines human issues of self-righteousness religious preachers, sexual desire, and people stuck in their narrow-minded cultural confines. The rain is, I think, a metaphor for the mentally unhealthy closeted way we all tend to become over time, blocked in by traditions, cultures, and values imposed on us by our upbringing.

The second thing that came immediately to mind when I looked out the window this morning and saw a typical heavy April shower was The Beatles song of that name. Music is part of me, inculcated by being the middle child in a large family, with older brothers and an older sister who all played music, from very early blues to sixties pop to the more experimental music of that time. "Rain", written by John Lennon, can be interpreted in different ways but at face value it's about how people moan about all sorts of weather, whereas for Lennon "Rain, I don't mind" and later "when it rains and shines, it's just a state of mind".

I think that both of these automatic reactions in my head to the word "rain" simply show that I have been culturally programmed through my life, in a harmless, some might say, fortunate way (though musical and literary tastes are absolutely a remarkably individualistic matter). If I had been born and raised in different circumstances I might not have had the opportunity, or indeed the artistic curiosity to even seek out such works of art. We are conditioned creatures, something mindfulness ask us to be explicitly aware of, and to watch out for the consequences of these.

The third thing that sprung to my mind was, predictably, the typical Scottish response to rain. "It's miserable weather". And yet. And yet.

When I went outside to feed our two rabbits in the heavy rain, I noticed that, because I was well dressed for the downpour it didn't affect me negatively at all. I saw a male blackbird in all its stark beauty drinking from a tiny water bowl we have for the birds, and two robins venturing near another bowl of water in the garden. And the flowers were out in all their radiant varieties of pastel and primary colours. And the trees, their bark dark and shiny with the rain, beginning belatedly to flourish with the warmer climate.

All of this only possible because of that "miserable weather".

I do a little personal practice related to water several times a day. Mindfulness practice states that we should aim to be aware of what is going on in each moment of our lives. So I notice what it feels like to feel the cold temperature of the water on my fingertips through the glass, and to be aware of the pleasure that signals in my mind. Then I move to the drinking itself, first the sensation of cool water on my lips, then its effect in my mouth – quenching, lubricating and cooling – finally a similar effect through the throat as I swallow. All of these successive sensations are pleasant, some beautifully so. The long-term effect of practicing these moments of pure mindfulness is that I feel a greater love of life, and this sticks. It become an ever-increasing part of me despite the woes of the world that we hear on the new each day. And this is not escapism. In a sense being obsessed by negative world news is a form of masochistic voyeurism because most of the time we can't or don't do anything about what we learn, except become impotently angry or despairing of our species. Meanwhile the joy of sipping water gets missed in the morass of our ruminations.

However, as someone who has been directly politically active, I do not passively accept all that happens in this world. I just approach it a different way. When I sip the water I deliberately add two mental processes to the experience of drinking.

Firstly I remember where the water came from. A series of pipes, connected at both ends to a water purification plant, then finally the pipes' origins at a reservoir.

I deliberately think to myself that in 1832 10,000 people in Scotland, of whom 3,000 were in Glasgow, died of the waterborne disease cholera, a disease which still kills 120,000 people a year around the world. From this I consciously cultivate appreciation for the society I live in which has structured itself in a way that enables us to drink this precious life-saving substance without any fear of death. My children grew up safe from the potential deadly impact of cholera and other waterborne diseases. I allow that appreciation to develop into gratitude for the pioneering scientists, thinkers and politicians who radically redesigned how we obtain water after the 1832 and subsequent cholera epidemics in our country.

Then I think of those who do not have clean water, even today. And I sow the seed of compassion in my mind as a result. Then I think of how my father, his sisters, all three just teenagers, and their mother, survived by sucking icicles that formed on their cattle trucks in order to stay alive. And the compassion grows because these are my nearest and dearest.

And it all comes down to rain, that precious, life-giving, life-saving substance. Think on it mindfully next time you see the rain fall. Practice, practice, practice.

Mental Poverty

We have some awful statistics about poverty here in Scotland. 17% of individuals are living in absolute poverty, this being defined as a condition where income is below that needed to provide the basics of life: food, clothing, shelter. The percentage for children is even higher, at 22% after housing costs.

People debate the causes of such poverty in the midst of increasing national and global wealth, and having delved into those debates for decades I sadly am no clearer as to how to end poverty than I was at the start. But there is another type of poverty that is rarely debated or even acknowledged. It exists amongst some, but not all of the financially poor, and it pervades every part of our society. I call it mental poverty.

The Buddha summed up what I mean. According to the ancient texts about his teachings he once said to his followers: There are two kinds of illness. Physical illness and mental illness. There seem to be people who enjoy freedom from physical illness even for a year or two, even all their life. But it is rare to find any individual who is free from mental illness, even for one moment.

At first glance, we might think, how bleak that is as an assessment of humanity. However he was viewing it from a very specific perspective. His definition of perfect sanity was that a truly free individual would not be controlled by their knee-jerk reactions, their negative mental habits, and their auto-responses to everyday things that normally irritate, frustrate or infuriate us.

This describes a mind that is happy, full of the joy of living, and able to deal with negative reactions without fuss or effort.

If this is a description of true mental wellbeing or mental wealth, how poor are we in comparison? Financial poverty often affects people's mental wellbeing. Perceptions of being socially excluded, labelled as failures or worse, build up of resentments and bitterness against a society that is evidently unjust, and other mental traits develop in many people who are on the lower rungs of our society's unhealthy version of a class system.

But I know many successful business people. Quite a few rich people. Many people who have been publicly praised. Many of them are mentally very poor. They feel that their work is shallow. It doesn't feed the deeper longings many people need in life. Some worry about their wealth. How it might be lost. Who is to get it when they die? How will it be divided? Who gets what? As for fame it becomes addictive to some individuals. Without the acclaim they feel hollow, empty, devoid of a self that is solid and content in its own right.

You may feel these are extreme cases but some of the most prestigious professions in Scotland have high levels of stress, unhappiness and depression. Ironically doctors have one of the highest rates of these symptoms of mental poverty compared to other careers.

Lawyers too. The stereotype of the ultra-cool, always confident legal expert in films and television programmes does not reflect a reality where many struggle with tiredness, lack of sense of fulfilment, even suicidal thoughts.

True mental health, as defined by the Buddha more than two millennia ago, is possible. As the old saying goes, we got into this mess, so we can get out of it. But it requires a radical shift in the way we think, communicate and act. And it requires us to let go of some of what our society so prizes in people. All that crap about ambition, success, status, acclaim, fame, praise, mega-wealth. These things are not just junk; they are, if we're not really careful, stumbling blocks to true fulfilment in life, and slippery slopes towards unhappiness and an unpleasant personality.

Mental poverty is simply the accumulation of myriad unhelpful experiences in your life. Therefore mental sanity and happiness are simply the opposite; the accumulation of myriad helpful and positive experiences in your life. Whether an experience is positive or negative depends to a great degree on how you perceive it, and this can be within your control, though it takes practice to be good at this.

Bad things happen in life. But is the death of someone you love a cause for ongoing lamentation, or a cause for great celebration of their life, and gratitude for all the years you had together? This is a choice we have.

As for fortune and fame, ignore the temptation to grasp at them. Instead learn what will fulfil and satisfy your deeper inner life, and do that, and if by some chance they do bring you fortune or fame, accept it but don't get attached to it. Treat it for what it is, a side-effect of doing what you really wanted to do.

Some people will argue that it is good to have drive and ambition, and that without it we'll all sink into mediocrity and apathy. But when we practice mindfulness and live according to its maxim of focussing on the present moment as much as we can, we actually get so much more done in life, without the draining, sapping effect of ambition and greed. You might actually find, as I did, that you end up achieving much more when you drop your goals and self-centred dreams than when you consciously pursued them.

So avoid the paths that lead to mental poverty, and follow deeper, more profound paths that truly sustain and nourish your finest mental riches.

What exactly is the present moment?

We live so much of our lives in thought. Often we say we are "lost in thought". It's such an apt expression, the wisdom of language showing itself. We ruminate, daydream, fantasise, worry, conjecture, regret. Meanwhile something called now is also happening, but because we are lost – in our thoughts – we don't make use of now. In that process we lose those moments for ever.

Estimates vary but around 70% of our automatic thoughts are negative. Related to this, a Harvard study showed that we are lost in our automatic thoughts for roughly half our waking day every day.

Common sense suggests that we will get the most out of our life if our mind is where we would choose it to be focussed on rather than where our automatic thought-production line drags us to, especially if most of them are negative.

Just one point of clarification. By getting the most out of our life I don't mean being driven like the stereotype Type A macho super-ambitious and egotistical business or political leader. I simply mean making the best use of each moment with a clear view of what a human being needs in their life in order to be happy, healthy and fulfilled. For most people that certainly does not mean being pushy or hard-nosed. In fact the opposite is usually more likely to lead to true happiness, good health and fulfilment.

To "be" in the present moment, we have to be aware of our thoughts and whether they are an obstacle or a help in this moment. If they are negative or distracting us from where we'd like to be mentally, then we can let them drop away simply by gently taking our attention to something neutral or pleasant like the freshness of an in-breath and the quiet calmness of the out-breath. That clears the mind and makes us more relaxed at the same time.

Then we have mental space and sufficient awareness to focus on what we want to do in that moment. If we have nothing specific then it is good mindfulness practice, and a way to simply enjoy being alive, to use any of our five senses to savour what is available to us in this precious moment.

I use the word precious because although we've had millions of moments, and hopefully will have millions more, each moment is fleeting and ephemeral, lost to us forever in an instant, so we should treat them as precious.

What do you see right now? Anything of beauty, comfort, interest, colour, design, style?

What do you hear? Birds singing, the wind blowing, cars slipping by, people at work, your own breath?

What do you physically feel? The air fill your lungs, or the same air slipping through your nostrils, your backside on a chair, the soft cotton of your clothes on your back, the subtle touch of air on the skin of your face?

Can you smell anything? Is it pleasant or unpleasant? If there is a smell allow the mind just to dwell on its pleasantness or unpleasantness for a moment, and let them mind just get the tiniest glimpse of the astonishing evolution of our body, brain, and this sense of smell that enables us to experience smells and distinguish ones we like from ones we don't.

If you'd like to eat, what do you actually taste? Taste is only one part of eating. What does your mouth feel? The heat or coolness of the food. The texture of the food when first put into the mouth. The change of texture as your teeth crunch and mash the food into digestible sizes. Alongside the taste is often the smell of the food. Does it complement the taste? What do we mean by complementing tastes and smells? How does the food look? Bland, colourful, varied colours?

Do you see what is possible in a moment? My old teacher, a monk in one of the many Tibetan schools of Buddhism, told me that reality is a field of potential. Reality is only possible in the present moment. The field of potential is what you can do in any moment with one or more of your five senses, plus your intellect and emotions. To continually just do whatever your automatic mind pops up with is to have no choice, no potential, no field to explore. Given that 70% of what it produces is negative, it's hardly likely to give you that lovely combination most people want, happiness, health, and fulfilment.

Try to think of your life as a game, a very serious game but still a game, the purpose of which is to stop your own automatic mind completely controlling your destination, and instead to make all you can of each moment. Try to see what is really possible in each moment. Can you turn a complaint into a positive suggestion? A bad memory into a commitment to change things in the future? Can you become someone who prevents negative things happening precisely because you stop being their cause?

These things are possible. Considered this way, every moment is an opportunity, a challenge, a canvas or blank sheet of paper on which you can create a work or art or poetry. This is not impractical or unrealistic. This is the whole point of being alive, to make full expression of the beauty of each moment.

Enjoying the Past in the Present

The old saying goes "familiarity breeds contempt" which I feel is a bit harsh. However familiarity does mean we often stop appreciating things. In fact we often stop noticing them at all at a clear conscious level. It's when other people, unfamiliar with the things we take for granted, comment on how special or wonderful something is, that we are reminded of an object's unique qualities. This is most commonly seen when people travel overseas to a completely new country or culture.

Those of us who live in Scotland and have done so most of our lives will acknowledge all the usual positive truths about our country. It is beautiful. We have several cities, towns and villages that are notably for their history, architecture, or vibrant contemporary regeneration areas. But the truth is, most of us see these things with a kind of acceptance rather than with the wow factor that someone new to the country sees it.

Some countries are predominantly arid. People from those countries who visit Scotland are amazed at how green our grass is. To which we think "it's just grass".

The same is true for our historic buildings, the contents of our museums and art galleries. If we are regular visitors it's always a pleasure to see the familiar exhibits. The dinosaurs, the Lewis chess pieces, Raeburn's skating minister, Dali's Christ of St John of the Cross, and anything and everything by Charles Rennie - and his wife, belatedly credited and still under-recognised Margaret Macdonald - Mackintosh.

We still see them. We still think they're really special. But do we see them afresh or is it with a bit of the "it's just grass" mentality.

I have the privilege of guiding people round the Scotland Street Museum on Saturday 2 June. I'll be doing it from a mindfulness perspective. Yet for me this means a strange, paradoxical cycle. I have to visit it beforehand to prepare how I'll approach this. This means I'm becoming familiar with each aspect. But my aim in doing so is – and here's the paradox – to clear my mind of its tendency to take things for granted through over-familiarity. So I'm re-familiarising myself with the museum in order to see precisely where and how I take it all for granted, so that I can, if you like, reboot my brain so it is capable of seeing things afresh, as if for the first time.

That's not an easy thing to do. We are automatically programmed, moment by moment, a process that continues through life, with many of our views becoming increasingly fixed and narrow over the years. This plays out in our mind in the world of the arts, history and culture. Rather than having an open, flexible, supple perspective on these matters, time and familiarity tend to fossilise us into predictable views, likes and dislikes.

Part of what I love most about the effects of practising mindfulness is that it slowly dissolves or chips away at these stuck ways of seeing.

This helps to liberate me from the conditioning and programming that has built up inside us all of my life. In its place is a wide open warm-hearted curiosity about things. Sure, my age-old prejudices do surface still, such as my liking for Joan Miro and Jean Arp but my dislike for Lucian Freud and Francis Bacon, but being aware of their presence in me, I can to a large extent let them drop away from my mind and see the works of these artists more freely.

The arts are the ultimate place where the eye of the beholder rules supreme. A critic can give a million reasons why this painting is a gem but that one is rubbish, but no one can tell you what to like and what you can't like.

The Scotland Street Museum is a classic case in point. A revered work of architecture, now a museum of the history of education, it combines artistry and social perspectives. The contrast between the then avant garde design of the building, its windows, it's stairs, with the reconstruction of classrooms from different eras of the twentieth century, can help pull us out of our pre-conceived notions of what life was like in those times.

Our views of the past are very often clouded in prejudices. Whether that's skewed memories of your own life, or how you view significant events in history such as, from a global point of view, the bombing of Hiroshima, or the American Civil War, or in Scotland, the Battle of Bannockburn, the Red Clydesiders, we tend to create our own narrative.

Moreover when it comes to history, unless it was fairly recent we can only take historians words for it, and historians often disagree about the significance of events, and sometime even what actually happened.

When we practice mindfulness what seemed fixed and certain slowly gives way to an ability to not only accept but feel free in uncertainty. Somehow this feels lighter that the weightiness of deeply held opinions and stances. The only time we are able to live is right here, right now. We should be able to live with it free from constrained views of the past, but we can also reframe the past in a looser, more constructive way so that the past helps us be more fully present in the moment.

The Human Mind and the Natural Environment

I recently received a very interesting survey from the global windows and blinds company Velux about the extent to which people now get outdoors. This wasn't about mountain climbing, hiking, skiing, or doing extreme sports. It meant quite simply, how often do we literally get out of our homes and offices into the wider world of the wind, fresh air, the sky, clouds, trees, grass.

The figures were startling. According to the report we currently spend 90% of our time indoors. This survey was not conducted only in Scotland or the UK, where one might argue the weather plays an inordinate role in persuading us to remain inside, away from the rain. It covered 16 countries around Europe and America.

The report quoted years of research which have conclusively shown that the quality of air indoors is significantly worse than outdoors, contrary to what most people think. This has an effect on our physical health and has been cited in the rise of asthma and other pulmonary conditions, especially amongst the young.

From a mindfulness point of view however there are further concerns with our indoors lifestyle. We have evolved over millions of years, the majority of which we spent almost entirely outdoors or sheltering in places which were only partially shut off from the outside world, in caves, tents, and similar basic places of refuge from heat, cold, rain and snow.

Moreover, every day when we awoke we had to go out into the world to find food and interact with other individuals and communities. In short we have evolved to be intimately and continually inter-connected with the natural world.

When we are indoors we are excluded from this natural world. Our minds, conditioned by eons of expectations of having nature around us all the time, react negatively to the absence of what nature brings to us.
How do we connect with this world we live in? Through our five senses and the reactions of our mind to these sensations.

What do we see indoors? Maybe a dozen or so walls, some with paintings or photos on them. Couches, beds, toilets, the usual stuff.

What do we hear? Whatever is on television, conversations, perhaps some music.

What do we touch? The laptop I'm typing this on, the feel of hot water when you have a shower, your backside on a sofa.

What do you smell? Not much.

What do you Taste? It Depends on What We're Eating.

Compare this with the outside world. Taste apart, the world of nature has an infinitely greater variety of things to see, hear, touch, and smell than indoors.

These literally stimulate the mind through the senses. Our evolutionary path has shaped our mind to enjoy, appreciate and often love certain sights and sounds of nature, such as the blue sky, the ever-changing shape of clouds, the movement of trees in the breeze, bird song, the sound of rustling leaves. This is a spectacle that can bring awe and wonder to the human deeper inner being that we are, and such deep, inexplicable feelings nurture our mental health and joy at being alive.

I recently had the privilege and pleasure of being in Mexico. I enjoy art and was able to see again the astonishing giant murals of Diego Rivera and Jose Clemente Orozco, and David Alfaro Siqueiros, and the pre-colonial, colonial and modern architecture of that remarkable country. But none of it, and nothing humans have ever made, even Machu Picchu, the Taj Mahal, the Mona Lisa, Picasso's Guernica, the Saturn 5 rockets which took man to the moon, none of this come close to the wonder of existence of life on this planet, and the seemingly infinite varieties of living things that we share the Earth with. In Mexico we saw coatimundis, racoons, turtles, tortoises, tropical fish, all in their natural environment, alongside wonderful types of birds, including a hummingbird less than a meter from my face. And that's without covering the many types of cacti, palm trees, fruits that we saw every day.

You don't have to go to Mexico to get this emotional bond with our fellow life forms. We have deer, foxes, robins, blackbirds, bluebells, hills, mountains, locks, burns, firths, seas and a hundred more forms of beauty almost at our fingertips.

But you have to be outdoors to connect. If you're not outdoors you don't experience connection with the wider world of life. That absence harms your mental health. It robs you, starves you of joy, of appreciation, of compassion for life.

Living mindfully is not just about noticing the maverick and often self-harming creations of the mind. It is about noticing what we have evolved to love about life, and much of this is about the world outside our doors. And it's not just about noticing what we love. It's about noticing that we are actually enjoying it, and in noticing this, determine to make the most of it. Why watch a robin in your garden for ten seconds then rush off to do something inconsequential because it just happens to pop up in your mind, when you could linger with the robin for another ten, twenty, thirty seconds. This is communing with nature. This is you being more fully alive, being part of the much wider panoply of existence of which we are but a tiny part. Life is a temporary matter so enjoy it while you have it.

Mindfulness in Schools

In some respects we could argue that the recent upsurge in interest in mindfulness has come rather late in the day for most of us. It is a skill whose sole purpose is to help us be better aware of each moment, and through getting better at this, we see our poor judgements, hasty reactions, harshness, and allow these to fall away before they explode out of our minds and cause unpleasant effects all around us, as well as inside us.

So when I came across mindfulness at the age of thirty-nine, some twenty years ago, I had by then already accumulated almost four decades of mental habits, traits, prejudices, and egotistical viewpoints. So in the past twenty years I've used my practice of mindfulness as diligently as I can, for the most part, dealing with the junk and nasty mental traits that I spent the first forty years developing. Of course I didn't deliberately or even consciously develop these unhealthy habits of mind. They emerged and grew in me through the combination of the genes I inherited from my ancestors, and all the life experiences that happened to me, most of which I had little or no control over.

As far as my own life is concerned therefore, I have spent four decades accumulating unhealthy ways of thinking and reacting – and hopefully some pleasant ones too – only to spend the following two decades trying to neutralise and undo these.

Wouldn't it have been so much better for me and those I come into contact with, if I had been practicing mindfulness from my early youth?

Had that been the case two great benefits would have accrued to me. Firstly I would not have soaked in anything like as many negative mental ways of thinking as I did, because my mindfulness practice would have helped me notice these as they started to arise in my childhood, and I would have learned how to let them go, and stopped them becoming embedded in my mindset.

Secondly I would therefore had much more free time in my mindfulness practice to nurture the positive mental qualities of life, including tolerance, non-judgemental, non-prejudicial thinking, an appreciation of all things in nature, a love of all life, and a joy of being alive, as well as the core mental disciplines of clarity of thought, calmness in all situations, concentration on what I want to do, and compassion for those who suffer.

I don't regret not having had this alternative past. Mindfulness quickly lets us see that regret is a waste of time. However my life has taught me that others would benefit immensely if they started to learn mindfulness at as early an age as possible.

I have taught mindfulness to inmates in several prisons – including Barlinnie, Greenock and Dumfries prisons in a five day spell last week. Nearly everyone in jail has experienced severe and complex upbringings, and a high percentage had mental health issues before they even committed their first criminal offence.

Being imprisoned itself exacerbates the mental turmoil, anger and despair of those in jail. From a mindfulness point of view, where the aim is to help people liberate themselves from their own worst accumulated mental traits, this makes the job much harder.

But these prisoners were once little children. They went to school. They went to school for twelve years, and in those twelve years, because of the ongoing destructive mental conditioning going on in their lives at home or in care, they got worse mentally rather than better, despite the best efforts of teachers and other professionals. This is an extreme version of how we all develop mental traits, some bad, some good. I'd argue that if all of us had been given skilled, sympathetic mindfulness training in each of years at school our mental lives would have been transformed for the better, and each of us would be much happier, more productive, and more compassionate and kind than we currently are. This would be good for us as individuals, as members of our families, as friends, as communities, and ultimately as societies, including in such seemingly unconnected areas as economic development, entrepreneurship and scientific research.

I have had the privilege of teaching mindfulness to all levels in the education system, from primary one pupils to post-graduate university students. The youngest children don't need to be taught in a radically different way to the adults. Kids get mindfulness. Most of them immediately appreciate the positive experience of silence.

They know their emotions pretty well by the age of four, and once explained, are fascinated by how these arise, how we get them, and the fact that we can learn how to deal with them moment by moment. It doesn't in any way take away from their necessary sense of fun and play, rather it adds to these, heightens the joy of games and friendship.

Many school teachers are now qualified to guide people in mindfulness, and many head teachers are hugely enthusiastic about bringing it in more and more to class settings. Imagine how expert a child would be if they were wisely and skilfully taught to really understand and master their own evolving mental traits. Imagine how, after seven years of primary education involving mindfulness day by day, these children go to the big world of secondary school, and the onset of adolescence. How much better would they handle these two pivotal developmental stages in their lives.

I am convinced that this is a vision that is realistic, highly affordable, and is both greatly needed and much wanted by those teachers and parents who know the subject in depth. So let's give our children and their children the tools to live wisely and lovingly.

Taking a Break

No matter how fit you are, how healthy your lifestyle is, the demands of life and the limitations of our body mean that we'll get tired at times during the day. Unfortunately our conscious mind tends to get the message quite a while after we first actually become tired. As a result we usually continue to do work or other activities while tired, making us more tired in the process.

The body can of course also become tired, usually when we do a lot of physical activity such as sports, running, gardening, or heavy lifting. But physical tiredness can often co-exist with mental alertness, the bodily exercise causing the brain to become more rather than less sharp. What interests me is mental tiredness.

Tiredness of the mind is a very interesting state. As with so many aspects of how we feel and who we are from moment to moment, the practices of mindfulness gives us deep insights, and raises even deeper questions. Why does the mind get tired? We can answer instinctively that it does so because we have overworked it. But that begs another question. How much work is too much work? Biologists and neuroscientists can explain the chemicals and pathways that are used or created or depleted when tiredness develops in our mind, but these don't explain why we feel this strange sensation we call tiredness.

What we do know is that it is debilitating. People who suffer from long-term conditions whose symptoms include chronic tiredness testify to the near full incapacitation of their daily lives when mentally exhausted. There's not enough mental energy to even want to do something, let alone the physical or mental energy to do it.

We need to learn to recognise our mental tiredness much more swiftly that we currently do, so that we can rest and recover before returning to our activities. I know from personal experience that such an approach, when I am sharp enough to notice and respond with a short break, results in a far more productive and enjoyable life than attempting to work through tiredness.

So the first skill to learn is to notice periodically how alert or tired your mind is. This is pure mindfulness, noticing what going on from moment to moment. It takes time to develop this trait of observation but it does develop.

Then when you notice you mind is somewhat depleted you have a few options that can help.

The first is to close your eyes. This is not because you are tired and hope to take a nap. Rather it is to remove all the potential visual distractions from your mind's view. With less to distract it, the mind gets more of a break.

My favourite technique is, with eyes still closed, to use awareness of my breath to help my mind recover from its fatigue. I use just a sing in and out breath. I let the breath slow down significantly, so that it feels almost like it is happening in slow motion. But it is done without any force or artificial effort. The breath just flows in lightly and softly, and as it does I create the word "clear" in my mind. The inner utterance of this word lasts the entire slow in-breath, which can take as long as ten to twenty seconds.

I then do something similar with the outbreath. As it starts to flow outwards I manage its pace so that it seems to seep out more than flow, again without any sense of pressure or force. This time I create the word "peaceful". I let this word stay in my mind during the whole period of the outbreath.

Finally I gently and slowly open my eyes again, and I feel refreshed. It only takes less than a minute yet it recharges my mind's batteries in a significant way.

This is my own method, which over the years I have found is more effective for me than any other techniques I've tried. That doesn't mean it'll be best for you. Mindfulness is not prescriptive because each person's mind is unique, and an individual's mind changes throughout the day, so a particular method will work better or worse for different people, and maybe work well at one part of the day but not be as effective at another time. In other words you have to try different things to see what help you specifically.

A more common way is of course to have a hot drink. It's so common we have even come to call such a time of rest at work our coffee break or tea break. With mindfulness the point of a tea or coffee break is not so much to catch up with colleagues or friends but to experience what you're actually doing, namely drinking the tea or coffee.

In winter we tend to do this more naturally than in other seasons. When it's cold we like to cup the mug in our hands, and enjoy the warmth from the drink as it spreads through the mug. We also tend to savour the first sip of the drink.

But then the mindfulness vanishes in a puff of distraction. We start thinking of other things, what we've got to do next when we return to our workplace, or what happened earlier in the day. By doing so we miss the rest of the drink, and we miss the restful, restorative qualities that we experience when we focus lightly but clearly on the drink, its smell, its temperature, its taste, and the feeling of the cup or mug.

So build up the skill of noticing when you are tired, and use mindfulness to help restore your energy levels more effectively and quickly.

Suicide

This is a subject I have held back writing about. There is a fine line in writing between helpful exploration of a topic, and exploitation of others' suffering. However I feel that some people may benefit from a short perspective on what mindfulness has to teach us about suicidal thoughts and actions. Last week we had suicides of the fashion designer Kate Spade followed by that of chef Anthony Bourdain. Prior to this here in Scotland we had the tragic death of indie singer and songwriter Scott Hutchinson of the band Frightened Rabbit, and even closer to where I live, the loss of three teenagers from the Wishaw area.

Every time a suicide is reported there is rightfully a demand that we do more about preventing future deaths. Charities get set up, most often by parents of those who have taken their own life, in the desperate hope that other parents and siblings and friends may avoid the lifelong agony that suicide of a family member brings. They urge people to come to their events, to talk about their feelings, and they lobby government to take practical steps to help reduce the fatalities. This is all deeply moving and noble, and I have tried to help such groups as and when I could.

But in my view there is a much deeper and larger approach to this awful issue. Put simply we are all not as mentally well as we could be. We are all somewhere on a spectrum whose far end is a strong suicidal or murderous impulse.

Ironically and pitifully we don't even look at what is at the other end of the spectrum. Consider just for a moment how happy, contented, compassionate, joyful and loving a human being could potentially become, then compare it with the wretched suffering of one who feels life is so painful or unbearable that they must end it.

Why we feel and think as we do is simply the result of just two sets of things. The first set is the genes we inherit. We get them from our parents, but they got them from theirs, and so on back to the beginnings of life. They are very influential in how we feel and what we think.

The second set of things that determine how we feel and think is every experience we have ever had, right from a moment when the brain is sufficiently developed in our womb.

It's nature and nurture. Genes and experiences. There's nothing else that can shape us to think and feel as we do. And it's very complicated. We now know that they genes and experiences interplay and influence each other, all of which affects our thoughts, feelings and behaviour in a constant, fluid way, moment by moment. So one moment we can be laughing, and in the next angry or moody.

My view is that we have been given the most astonishing, brilliant but complex and volatile tool yet discovered.

But we have been given no instruction manual. Religion and philosophy used to try to do that job. Religion did so in a dictatorial way. I still remember my Catechism from the age of four or five. Who made me? God made me. Why did God make me? God made me to know him, to love him, and to serve him in this world so that I may be happy with him forever in Heaven.

Religions and philosophies have had to adapt dramatically to scientific discoveries. The old instruction manual needed updated.

In my opinion we need a new instruction manual, and we all need to learn it for our own good and for the good of those around us. Suicide is not just a tragic loss of an individual's gift of existence. It has a horrific and hugely debilitating effect on those closest to the victim. Yet life is all we have, and looked at through a different lens, can legitimately be seen as an inexpressibly beautiful and awesome experience. This is the view from the other end of the spectrum. But we need a manual to move along that spectrum in the right direction.

What happens in many people's lives is that they move along the spectrum, but in the wrong direction. Biologically we have a built-in negativity bias. We are more likely to see things negatively than positively, and certain aspects of our society logically reflect that bias and magnify it.

The news media purports to tell "the news" but actually it tells only the tiniest part of what happens in life, and focuses almost exclusively on bad news or crises.

So we have developing in our heads a vicious circle of negativity bias being constantly fed by a daily stream of negative stories which claim to be an accurate summary of what's happening in our world.

We all need to arm ourselves against this unnoticed but relentless drift to the negative end of the mental spectrum, and we need to not only do that but work our way slowly, steadily and optimistically towards the other end of the spectrum.

This should be a societal priority, not a minor sticking plaster. None of us is predetermined to become suicidal. Each of us has the potential to be resiliently happy, powerfully loving and compassionate, and deeply infused with a sense of joy at being alive. In every country in the world not just here in Scotland, we are so far adrift from that potential we are all failed states. The purpose of life, and therefore of all societies, is to live it richly, and to love the living of it. This should be our national vision, and from it the strategic and operational work to achieve it should logically follow. All life is too precious to allow even the thought of suicide to enter a person's mind. Let's get serious about living our lives.

The Delusion of Identity

So it's World Cup time, and as you read those words you will have a reaction to that tournament which may vary from enthusiasm to instant dislike. Around the world people from the 32 countries taking part will already have had moments of joy and woe, of thrills and fears, all centred around a couple of dozen men running around a field kicking a ball.

We like to support our team if they're taking part. Some countries' involvement mean nothing to us. Others we may actively dislike because of their regime or government or historical events. Russia is the host nation. I have a friend who is not watching the tournament because Russia is hosting. He likened it to Hitler's Berlin Olympics in 1936. He is Polish.

It's like the Eurovision Song Contest where you can predict one country's vote for another, depending on how friendly or unfriendly these two countries have been through history.

Will England fans support Argentina, with the Falklands still in people's memories, and Maradona's hand of God incident against England in 1986? For that matter Scots have not traditionally wanted England to do well in the World Cup.

This is all about identity. About who we deem ourselves to be, and about the mental invention of a sense of me, us, and others. So who am I, the person who is writing this?

In terms of national identity my immediate thought is, I am Scottish. I was born in Cambuslang, Scotland. I was raised here and spent most of my life living in Scotland. I speak with a Scottish accent. Anyone with a passing understanding of Scotland and the Scots would immediately on meeting and hearing me think I'm Scottish.

The fact that my name and my father are Polish doesn't count. My mother, born in Scotland to parents also born in Scotland, is however one hundred percent Irish in her genes, going back to when Thomas Murphy left Ireland in the 1840s. So in terms of my DNA I don't have a single atom of Scottishness in my body.

Interestingly had this been the exact same scenario but my ancestors had hailed from a country where people's skins were not what we call white, people may have viewed me differently. My accent could be the same. My depth of understanding of Scottish life, culture, history, and geography could be just the same, but somehow in the minds of many, though not all, I wouldn't be really Scottish, or I'd be Scottish but only after they had thought about it. They wouldn't think I'm what I'd call Scottish Scottish or Really Scottish.

It's interesting that my Polish and Irish labels are rendered invisible by an accent and the colour of my skin.

Labels are useful and necessary but we have to be careful or they start to define us in narrow, exclusive terms. Labelling others is also useful and necessary, but the same caveat applies.

Just like an axe is useful, we don't want to just leave it lying around because it is potentially dangerous. Treat your labels and labelling with care.

What does it actually mean to be Scottish, British, European? This is an important question but as soon as it is raised it becomes loaded with political implications and suggestions. The very fact that I raise it as a theme in this column might cause all sorts of people to think I am trying to send a political message, that I'm a crypto-nationalist, a narrow-minded British unionist, or a Remainer.

We are all accidents of birth and circumstances. You who are a pro-Union Brit, or a pro-independence Scot, a pro-EU European, or an anti-EU European. or any other label you like to attach to yourself, could, with a simple twist of fate, have been Canadian, Spanish, Thai. And if so, you might view yourself as none of these labels. You might not even know or care about the seemingly trivial politics of Scotland, British and Europe. Your mind and political labelling would be focussed elsewhere.

You are not who you think you are. These labels are all just conditioning, and the conditioning is just the result of pure chance. You didn't choose your parents but you got your genes, which are like computer programmes, some set from conception at ON, others at READY but requiring life experiences to either switch them on or keep them switched off.

Amongst these genes are ones which seem to deeply influence our political persuasion. So your dearly-held national and political labels may be the result of nothing more than a bit of chemistry triggered by a couple of passing experiences.

This is easy to understand intellectually. You just need to read a credible book, check out the research and you get it. But at an inner level it's an entirely different matter. Most of us are so deeply and emotionally embedded in our understanding of our sense of self, of what we are, and what we're not, that what I am writing about here represents a profound, and seemingly threatening and dangerous challenge to your deepest views about yourself. All of our views about ourselves are just a bunch of prejudices, a set of delusions created my that fascinating and mysterious combination of genes and chance life experiences. So, keep your labels if you feel you need them, but wear them very lightly, and don't let them harm you or those around you. And enjoy what's left of the World Cup.

Using your Heritage

Mindfulness is structured around the fact that we are only alive in the present moment. The future isn't here yet, so all we can do is imagine, hope, or worry about it. The past, meanwhile has already gone, so what we do with our mind is remember, reflect and often ruminate about what has already happened.

So where does your heritage come into this philosophy? We have an unbreakable bond with our family and our ancestors. When you stop to think about it, all you are is an aggregate of genes and life experiences. The genes you received from your parents, and they affect you enormously, even if you happened to be adopted at birth so never had experiences living with your parents. Still, their genes help to shape who you are and who you will continue to become, because "who you are" doesn't stop changing and evolving through your life.

On top of this every experience you had with your parents, siblings, grandparents, cousins and so on also had and still has an impact on who you are and how you behave and react in everyday life.

So there's no getting away from family. The question, from my perspective, is, what we can and should do about this profound, deeply personal part of our life.

I tend to use it to nurture two healthy mental qualities, and also therefore, combat two unpleasant mental states that can otherwise unwittingly grow in our minds. The two positive qualities are gratitude and compassion, and the negative opposites are taking things for granted and indifference to the suffering of others.

In a very bitter ironic twist I am lucky to have much in my Polish ancestry to use to nurture both gratitude and compassion. Compared to how their lives went, mine is so easy, so fortunate, so safe.

There's not the space to go through all the details so here's just some of it. My grandmother died of starvation and exhaustion. My father and his sisters were deported to the labour camps of the Soviet Union. My dad had typhus, dysentery twice, and malaria all in a single year. My aunt weighed three stone, twelve pounds at the age of fifteen. My grandfather died of cancer while serving in the Polish underground army, bereft of his wife and children for the last four years of his life. Five of his seven siblings died in infancy. His parents and his Stepek grandparents never made it past forty years old, all falling to tuberculosis. One of my father's cousins was captured by the Soviets and was murdered with a bullet to the back of his head in a basement cell. He was twenty one years old. His brother is still alive, still mourning. Another of my father's cousins died of typhus in Kazakhstan.

That's the bare bones. I've left out the other family members who were taken to Soviet labour camps or the dreaded Nazi concentration camps in Germany.

And I've left out the lifelong chasm all these events caused between the broken family members, and between the large number who found themselves in exile from their homeland for the rest of their lives.

How do we begin to imagine what those poor people went through? We can't. But we can feel. We can feel compassion and love for them just through a little mindful attention on the enormity of their suffering. Just paying attention to the magnitude of their life experiences can open up in us these necessary and healthy sensations.

However it is important not to allow such powerful emotions to turn negative, into anger, pessimism, or despair. So we need to have mental discipline to keep the emotions healthy and directed towards our empathy for those who suffered, not the people who caused their pain. How to deal with that is for another time, not now. Right now we are deliberately nurturing love and compassion.

We can then let this compassion spread outwards to others who suffer, especially those who are suffering right now in our own time. This not only increases our capacity for compassion but prevents the otherwise natural mental tendency to become more self-centred and tribal in our thinking about others.

And then to gratitude. I do a little practice when I drink cool water, in addition to noticing the beauty of the coolness, the freshness of the water, the lubricating and cooling effect it has on my mouth.

I think of my grandmother and my father and my aunts shrivelling from lack of water, their mouths parched, fearing death. And I deliberately bring to mind pure undiluted gratitude for living in such a special place that has water running almost freely to all of our homes and workplaces, pure and clean and life-sustaining. Also that I live in a place where I am relatively speaking free from fear, safe, secure, unlike many of my direct ancestors.

If you are truly mindful of your current situation, unless you are in exceptionally unusual difficult circumstances, you can start to see just how privileged and fortunate we are to live as we do today. In all of human history people had no guarantee until recently that the precious life-sustaining water we all need would be safe to drink. Homes were not centrally heated, roads were mud-strewn, cars and planes did not exist.

Let your mind settle from time to time, and allow these insights of compassion and gratitude to arise and grow in you when we you think of your family history.

What is Justice?

Last week I attended two great events on the theme of women and the justice system. By coincidence both were on the same day, one in Hamilton, the other in Glasgow. Their times overlapped so I missed a bit of each but think I got the gist of both.

One thing especially made an impact on me. I can't remember the speaker but they said something along the following lines, echoing to some extent the narrative in the song made famous by Elvis Presley, In The Ghetto, a song whose original title was The Vicious Circle.

A child grows up in chaotic or troubled circumstances, perhaps involving violence at home, alcohol or drug use by their parents, various forms of abuse or neglect, and a home where culture, the arts and the things that make a human flourish are missing.

As a result that child is unruly at school or absent from it, turns to alcohol and drugs at an early age, creates trouble as a way of gaining status to fill the void of self-esteem in their heart, and eventually their behaviour cross over from the distracting and unpleasant to the criminal.

They are taken to court several times for different offences and are eventually jailed.

So following that dismal chain of cause and effect we can logically claim that we have punished a person because they were beaten, abused, neglected and prevented from learning how to enjoy a full life. We have jailed them for the harm caused to them by their early life.

None of this is to argue that dangerous people should not be prevented from hurting others, but it is an argument to say that punishment should not be part of the culture or thinking of our society because it ignores the very reasons why most people do harmful things.

Moreover it is an argument to say that we should drop words that have been soaked in judgemental and punitive terms for millennia, including the word justice itself. Justice is an inherently subjective opinion hence it has no right in what should be an inherently objective exploration of what to do about someone who has caused harm.

Humanity is very belatedly learning as fact what many of our greatest thinkers have suggested through the ages. Jesus said Judge not that ye be not judged, and even more powerfully, Let he who is without sin cast the first stone. The Buddha's teachings on karma and the human mind is that absolutely everything is simply the result of cause and effect and that there is no separate self in a person who makes decisions. Everything and everyone is conditioned.

If you don't believe this, ask yourself why you can read English. Its conditioning by your parents or learning it at school or as a result of coming to Scotland.

Those conditions led you to know English as a language. Some people, unlucky, unfortunate, learn the absence of love, the development of hate, the language of violence and fear as a way of being. They are victims, and don't have the skillsets to combat these tendencies without some form of recalibration of their mind. Tragically many may have minds so twisted and skewed that they reject the very help offered to them. I've been in Barlinnie, Shotts, Greenock, Dumfries, Castle Huntly, and Low Moss prisons teaching mindfulness to prisoners. Some can get what I teach, other can't, or at least, aren't able to at that stage in their lives.

Yet hope really does spring eternal. People do change, dramatically, for the better, though it can take a very long time.

This way of thinking, or perpetrators as themselves victims, goes against the historical grain of our culture. Many of our judges' pronouncements in the past have seemed to emerge more from the harshness of the Old Testament, fire and brimstone, hell fire, and all that, rather than the New Testament's Father forgive them for they know not what they do. We don't realise the sheer scale of our own conditioning, the centuries of a mindset of good versus evil, absolute free will, therefore absolute reasonableness of punishment, the desire for societal vengeance, a kind of justice as community lynching.

That's going, slowly, but it's going.

For most of us this may be an academic matter only. Most people are not victims of major crimes nor have their loved ones been incarcerated for committing crimes. Where this is directly relevant is in how we judge ourselves.

We are often brutal in our self-criticism. We tell ourselves we are able to learn such and such a skill, people like us can't go to university because we didn't do well at school, we never forgive our own past wrongful actions and so we live with guilt and self-loathing for the rest of our lives.

We are wracked by this insane, poisonous and harmful state of mind, which is an identical but microscopic version of the societal mindset I have just described. It does no one any good at all. It only harms. Individuals cannot enjoy life fully because this junk weighs them down, and society cannot properly heal and recover and flourish because we are so dragged downwards by wrongly perceived and constructed notions of culpability and responsibility for our actions.

Start with yourself first. Notice your tendency to judge yourself. Notice your tendency to judge others. See how powerful and woeful it all is. Practice the difficult bot doable skills of letting it go when it arises, or subtly deflecting it by switching your attention to the clearer and gentler sensations of your own breathing. Sounds too simple to work doesn't it?

Try it. You'll be surprised.

A Thousand Opportunities

When I first discovered mindfulness back in the late 1990s my Tibetan Buddhist teacher at the time taught me a phrase which I have used ever since. Reality is a field of potential. At first it seemed just like one of those New Age, Eastern spiritual quotes that suggest a lot but actually don't make sense when examined.

But I pondered it over the years. At the same time I dropped or adapted aspects of my Buddhist teachings, and added the latest neuroscience findings and psychological insights into the mix of what is now the secular form of mindfulness that I teach.

Over time the phrase started to be reworked in my brain.

Reality is a field of potential.

Reality, we are constantly reminded in our mindfulness practice, only exists in the present moment. Therefore the phrase can be reworded as The present moment is a field of potential. That struck me as less abstract, and of greater practical application in my life.

But I had still to decipher or clarify what the field of potential meant.Then the wonders of the human brain came to help. When we practice mindfulness and study the science that it rests upon, we start to see that in most everyday situation our mind works automatically, that is, it creates moods, emotions, reactions and thoughts without our conscious input.

It's more like the music app Spotify's option of Shuffle Play. This allows you to choose an album but the app then randomly chooses which song gets played one after another.

If we don't intervene on our mind's creations of feelings and thoughts then we have no choice. We are, in those moments, the slave of our automatic mind. But if we are mindful, we can notice this automatic mental production run as it occurs, and if we feel that what the mind has produced is not healthy or appropriate at that time we can let the thought go.

Then all of a sudden everything opens up, wide and deep and fresh and alive. We are no longer on automatic. This means we can choose amongst a million options in the next moment. Do you want to sing? Dance? Stay quiet? Look at the trees outside? Check your emails? And so on.

This is the field of potential in the phrase above. The field represents the infinite choices we now have available to us. We are liberated for a moment from our automatic mind and what is produced. The potential means, with clear thinking, we have the potential to create something special in this new moment of our life.

With kindness we can make someone's day in the moment. With intelligence we can solve a problem or help make a situation better. With creativity we can write a poem, sketch something of beauty.

Which brings me to a beautiful new book which I'm still reading. It's a called The Mindful Day by Laurie J Cameron. As some of you may know by now I am pretty fussy when it comes to books of any genre. Most seem to me dry, unoriginal, often lacking in insight or passion. The Mindful Day is a joy to read. It combines a flowing narrative with clear explanations of what being mindful is like in real life. It covers the science in a neat way, sprinkled through the book so that it remains relevant to the topics covered chapter by chapter.

It is also an easy read, structured as a series of short chapters most of which are only four to five pages long, and each chapter has a How? section giving examples of ways to try to bring mindfulness into that aspect of your day.

Laurie has worked with some of the world's largest corporations so a fair amount of the book covers how to be mindful at work. She does so in a refreshing, open way, recognising common negative traits most of us feel at times in the workplace. Boredom at meetings, loss of focus at the desk, stress and tiredness and all the things you have personally experienced.

She also covers important parts of our life that are increasingly squeezed out by our use of technology and mass entertainment. The joys of personal relationships, and our innate connection with the natural world are movingly covered, as are the benefits of doing these things with a quiet sense of attention, appreciation and gratitude.

The books covers from the moment we wake up to our last thoughts at night, and most of what we would normally do in between. There are so many suggestions and practices in the book that I'd caution you to start with one or two, build them into habits first, then slowly but surely add on more and more, so that your life becomes intertwined with your mindfulness practice. Ultimately in my view that's what true mindfulness is, just living your life more fully, more appreciatively, more altruistically and joyfully precisely because you are mindful of what life offers moment by moment. Mindfulness is not a set of practices you do whilst you take a pause from real life. Mindfulness is living real life properly.

So I'd very highly recommend this book, and hope you work with it to nurture your mindfulness qualities as well as enjoy the reading of it.

So back to reality as a field of potential. You have moments, thousands of them each and every day. Each one gives you a potential choice; to do whatever your mind randomly creates in that instant, or, with the help and insights gained from Laurie's book, to transform each one into something better, something special, something worthy of this precious life we have.

Avoiding Social Media Traps

I found myself inadvertently caught up in one of those emotionally charged social media threads the other day. I won't even dignify the original perpetrator, nor the subject, for that would be to keep alive a flame of hatred that doesn't deserve another moment's publicity.

I'll give a general summary of what happened. There had been a major news item. I checked it out on Twitter. Looking through the latest news and views about it, I came upon a hate-filled inuendo about a section of our society. It really doesn't matter which section of society – gender, race, sexual preference, football team, religion – because the hatred applied is always just a variant on the same theme.

My mistake was to be drawn by the hateful comment to see how others responded to it. As you can imagine there were comments on both sides. Some who disagreed with the original comment vilified the person who wrote it. Others agreed with the prejudiced comment and added their own for good measure.

I didn't reply, which was in my opinion, a good thing. One more comment in an avalanche of views makes no difference. Each side is already converted. Besides, any comment I made would have produced another lot in response, which I would probably read in due course, agreeing with some, disagreeing with others. The ones I'd disagree with would rankle in my mind for several minutes, maybe longer, disturbing my peace of mind, to no positive effect whatsoever.

In fact that's what happened without me even getting further involved.

Immediately after I read the thread of comments I went out for a short walk around the block, something I try to do hourly or so in order to get some fresh air, destress my mind, exercise my body, and enjoy some peace of mind by noticing the views, the sounds and the feelings associated with taking steps.

The walk usually only lasts seven or eight minutes, but for at least half that time my mind was suffering. It was trying to work out what one could realistically do with this person who made the inflammatory comment. To say it ruined the whole point of my walk would be an exaggeration. But it certainly poisoned much of it.

This article you could say is my attempt to not only salvage some purpose to my walk, but more than that, to create something positive, helpful and pleasant out of it. My conclusions were reached well after the inner pain and anger had completely subsided. My clearer and calmer thoughts were, I think, likely to have been produced by my mind even if I had never had the initial negative experience of reading the unpleasant comment in the first place. I know this because I have had previous similar thoughts about social media without the negative stimulus.

My view is clear. Try never to get caught up in such toxic matters, no matter how much you feel about the subject or the incident it refers to.

There are in equal measure professional and political provocateurs online, whose sole purpose is to ignite strong reactions in order to propagate a political view in the case of political firebrands, and for money in the case of "professional" writers and personalities.

If we don't read their initial comments they are starved of the flames that send their destructive messages further. Just as mindfulness tells us about our own negative mental traits, let them fall by the wayside without influencing you in any way. You don't feed your negative traits, so slowly but surely they become weaker and less frequent, and therefore much easier to handle.

It's the same with the social media stimulators of hate. If they get no response, they get no reward, political or financial. Moreover, not indulging them in the opportunity to make further comments means they have less chance to feed their own hateful mental habits.

This begs a bigger question of how we are to relate to the media more generally, including news programmes on television or radio as well as social media, and of course the newspapers, including this one.

I have followed the news since I was a kid, but seriously from my early twenties. I am still a habitually checker of the news and political activities.

However, because of the development my mindfulness practice has given me of awareness of my own feelings from moment to moment, I now know just how much absorbing the news and political produce drains and irritates me. My political views have not changed at all since I was a teenager, and are highly unlikely to change in the latter part of my life.

So all of my listening to, watching, or reading political news and comments, unless they were enjoyable to do, are a complete waste of my time. Moreover they are not only not enjoyable, but rather unenjoyable, and cause all sorts of negative states in my mind that I consciously don't want to be there.

We feel there is a need to keep up to date with "the news" but the news is simply a biased edited selection of the most sensational recent events, probably less than one in a million things that happened in the preceding twenty four hours. So it's not an objective choice and it's not representative of what life is actually like. In short in my opinion it adds absolutely nothing to your life and we'd all be better off without it.

That said, I still indulge, but much more carefully and much less frequently. My addiction is fading but it hasn't yet gone, and I am definitely thinning out my social media activities.

See the Whole Spectrum

We are programmed to think in terms of black and white. Something is either good or bad. We support one team and dislike another. We love a certain television programme but don't like something else. I think that we have evolved to be like this because it makes life simpler to traverse. Just ignore the stuff you don't like, and stick to what you do, and everything becomes more certain in your mind. This gives us a reassuring illusion of safety and security, a stability from which to live our lives.

It doesn't help us however. Life is not binary, good and bad. Life is complex, so complex we barely really understand it, least of all how our own minds work. So it helps if we can become much more fluid and open in the way we perceive things. That way we don't get floored when reality comes and hits us with a crisis or tragedy.

If we deliberately try to see things as parts of a spectrum we can learn to stop being quite so judgemental. This enables us to start to see the bigger picture of how we are. Let's take the topical issue of mental health as an example. For decades when people, especially people in the medical professional and in politics, talked about mental health they usually meant mental illness, and almost always equated the term mental health with poor mental health.

This was such a prevalent mindset in the profession of psychology that the paradigm of "positive psychology" was promoted by Martin Seligman only as recently as 1998. Yet positive psychology is not some rare condition. It simply refers to something we all know is true every day, namely that we experience positive, healthy, enjoyable emotions as well as negative ones.

Every one of us can rhyme off words that describe what is at the negative end of the spectrum of mental health. Suicidal thoughts. Raging anger. Hopelessness. Sadism. Cruelty. Self-harming. These remain major issues for far too many people in our society, yet the words and conditions those words represent have been recognised and treated in various ways through all of human history.

This is not the case at all at the other end of the spectrum. What words describe that positive extreme end of the spectrum? Love, kindness, happiness, contentment, calmness, peace of mind, joy, laughter. How little effort have we made to explore how we become positive and mentally vibrant and well, compared to the negative strand of our mental continuum?

We need to recognise that almost no one is stuck at a single point on this spectrum, especially at the negative end. We need to update our understanding of one another so that we recognise that we are all fluid beings who are sometimes morose, other times cheerful, and that this change can happen in an instant.

Fluidity is in fact a much better way of describing the reality of who we are than the fixed image we have of our self in our own minds. The Buddha once said we are more like a river than a solid being, constantly in flow and change. Once you grasp this deeply, it helps enormously with the real purpose of life which in my opinion is simply to enjoy that flow and those changes.

Every human being travels along lines of behaviour and attitudes. A shy person can grow out of that shyness and become a confident outgoing type. A murderer can stop being murderous, or perhaps was only every murderous in feeling and intention once, for a solitary moment.

When we start to think of people as changeable in any direction, and behaviours and moods and states of mind as temporary in each of us, then we are getting closer to the truth of how life actually is.

This growing awareness also helps us see our own prejudices and unfair likes and dislikes in the glare of true and deep observation. We start to see the problem with labelling people. We see how wrong it is to lump everyone from a particular group, race, religion, class, or political party as all being the same, when we see that not even one individual remains the same from minute to minute. The whole simplistic construct we make about others crumbles when viewed in a truer light.

Although it makes it much harder for our poor wee lazy brains, we come to recognise that we simply can't label people, whether we're talking about an individual or a group of individuals.

Life is much richer and harder to pin down than our automatic mind wants it to be. The brain that has evolved to constantly try to seek order and simple understanding in everything it encounters needs to be trained to come to terms, then to be happy with the mercurial nature of not just our own species but of all forms of life.

The truth is, nothing about life forms is simple, and nothing about this planet we live on is simple. It's all remarkable and complex and surprising and stunning if we can overcome our blinkered perspective that has slowly but surely grown inside us over the course of our lifetime.

So try to develop, day by day for the rest of your life, an ever-increasing rejection of stereotyping and labelling, and nurture instead a way of seeing everything as a much more fluid, flowing and changing swirl of what I can only call stuff, because there is no word to truly explain it.

Learned Behaviour

Some things we get from our parents via their genes. The image of your face, whether you are left or right-handed, maybe even your political tendencies.

Other things we learn through experience. The language or languages you speak. You weren't genetically programmed to speak English. If fate or chance had it otherwise you might be speaking and writing German or Japanese or any other language today.

We learn so many things through absorbing our experiences that we don't even notice that that's all they are. Learned behaviour. Learned choices of activities. Learned ways of thinking. Learned likes. Learned dislikes. That's just how the human brain works. We have experiences, the brain collates them, and the result is our traits and habits and ways we think.

You may be a person who flies off to Thailand and saves children's lives in a cave. That's learned behaviour. You weren't born to want to do that, nor with the skills to do it successfully.

You may be a person who goes on Orange, or Irish Republican, walks, or supports them from the pavement. Alternatively you may be a person who hates those who go on such walks or supports them in any way. Note that, whatever your view, you were not born to do that or to think in that way.

You simply acquired those views and those activities through life experiences. Consider for just a moment. Had you happened to be adopted when a baby by parents who thought the opposite to the people who raised you - you might have the total opposite view about the Catholic-Protestant divide in Scotland to the one you currently have.

Do think about this. It's a tough thing to consider but it is healthy to do it. It means that all of our opinions, every single one of them, is not a result of our brilliant reasoning, or the "right view" but rather past conditioning by life itself. Even our ability to reason is itself conditioned by past experiences and our genes.

The key question then arises. What is healthy behaviour?

I don't just mean the obvious physical health activities, like being careful about what you eat and drink, exercising enough to keep your heart and lungs healthy, and doing enough to keep your muscles relatively strong. Most of us know that stuff, even if we don't always do it.

I mean behaviour that results in us having a happy and open-hearted state of mind, and behaviour that doesn't hurt and upset others. In other words I think being mentally healthy is about being happy, at peace, and not wishing harm on others.

Understand this deeply. Then we start to see that so much of what we do every day is done mindlessly, with no thought at all to whether this use of our time is healthy for us or for those around us.

Let's look at a personal example. I watch the news in the morning if I have time and I watch it again at six o'clock in the evening. At the evening viewing I watch the BBC News followed immediately by Reporting Scotland, so this takes up an hour of my time almost every day.

What do I get out of this? A very small set of stories about what's happening around the world. The majority of it is about political or economic matters, and serious crimes. If instead I decided just to scan the BBC news website on its World, UK, and Scottish pages I could get the gist of it all within ten minutes.

That would give me fifty minutes extra every single day.

I think watching the news gives me nothing of value at all. You may disagree, but for the sake of this piece just bear with me for now. Healthy behaviour is behaviour that does me no harm, does no harm to others around me, and maybe does some good for both me and others.

Let's imagine that instead of watching an hour of the news I write another article like this -every day – and share it with people.

Firstly I actually enjoy writing. And it makes me think about how I live my own life. It also hopefully makes others think, which I would say is good behaviour. It might even makes one or two people change their own fixed behaviours from unhealthy to healthier, which is a good thing for them.

Or I might decide to go for a walk in the local park. Every day. That's good for my physical health, getting good moderate exercise, and strengthening my legs, core and back a little. And it's good for my mental health, getting fresh air and being in nature.

The ideal direction for all of us would be to gently and in a kindly way assess all of our mental and physical habits as they arise, note them all down, and decide that slowly but surely we will work on letting go of each of the ones we feel do not nurture our own wellbeing or the wellbeing of those around us.

This can take a lifetime but the alternative is to stick with a bunch of ways of thinking, reacting and doing that we know hurts us and those around us. So any progress we make on any one or more of our conditioned negative habits is a good thing. Moreover as each one diminishes we replace it with truly nurturing ways of thinking, responding and doing, so that our life gets better and better.

Mindfulness and the Big Bad World

Over recent years there have been suggestions by some commentators that those engaged in mindfulness are not critical of, or avoid any attempt to change the destructive aspects of the corporate world.

Every single one of the people I know directly or indirectly who bring mindfulness to the big corporates do so in the hope and belief that it will help to change the culture of those organisations to be fairer, more humane and less inherently destructive. It seems to me that it is only those on the outside who assume that this is not the case.

Some will rightly argue that changing the culture of a few companies might be fine for their employees but doesn't change the perceived cancer at the heart of the neoliberal mindset under which we all have to live.

That's right. But to be fair and balanced we should ask ourselves, what else has changed or does change the neoliberal culture? Communism tried. Look at the results. My grandmother dead in a grave some 1800 miles away from her home as the crow flies, one of just over a hundred million citizens known to have been killed by that experiment in creating a better society. Or how about democratic socialism under Labour in Britain? Why did people not buy into it enough to re-elect them after the seismic 1945 government, or the Wilson periods in the 1960s and 70s?

Look even the most highly regarded countries in the world with regards to social security and equality, the Nordic countries. The lands of IKEA, Nokia, Lego, mass oil and gas exploitation. Have they or anyone else found the alternative? Why then do some demand that mindfulness does what no other way of doing or being or governing has managed it? We are not measuring the right thing when judging mindfulness.

What does change life, cultures and countries are human minds. We have limited control over external natural factors such as weather, seasons, and natural disasters, but we do have the potential to better manage and direct our minds. The neoliberal world which we all condemn but we all literally buy into, the consumer society which we know is the cause of so much that is destructive, both globally and mentally, is something everyone I know participates in to a greater or lesser extent, and mostly to a greater extent, all the while, while condemning it.

If human minds got us into this mess, it can only be human minds that can get us out. Our thoughts become our words and our actions. Wrong-minded thoughts can become wrong-minded words and wrong-minded actions. Result? Suffering, inequality, greed, indifference, hatred, consumerism, climate change.

Right-minded thoughts become right-minded words and right-minded actions. Result? Reduced suffering, greater equality, altruism, compassion, activism, restraint of consumption, hopefully an end to increased climate change.

Note that if there's no thoughts there are no human-created problems. All our manmade problems originate in thoughts. So it's thoughts we have to sort.

Mindfulness is a discipline that asks us to notice what's going on, and in doing so asks us to question our mindsets and thoughts. It allows us to pause the communications and actions we do, and assess how these might affect each other, the world, including how we vote and how we accept or seek to change how life is structured right now. This is because mindfulness is not directive; it is not socialist or anarchist or libertarian or authoritarian or neoconservative or liberal. It is observational, and from observation, especially observation of our genetic and life-experiential skews and biases, we can rethink more clearly and more objectively and more deeply how things are, how we think things might become better, and how to make the most effective steps in those directions. That doesn't mean our conclusions are always right but it helps us move in that direction.

As for the Buddha in all this? He created mindfulness in an attempt to bring peace and control over his own thoughts. He then started to teach it to help reduce people's suffering, so it was an altruistic and compassionate motive from the start. According to the stories he mediated between warring tribes and nations, helping to end wars. He linked two things together; how individuals could stop suffering, and how societies could become better.

He taught ten duties for rulers, even advice for employers, including giving away their wealth, not cheating or harming, giving up personal comfort, being honest and kind, living a simple, frugal life, promoting peace and non-harming. How can such a philosophy be viewed as compatible with consumerism and the neoliberal way we live?

So when people say mindfulness is a lackey of the corporate world they're not talking about mindfulness, but something else. Call it McMindfulness or any label you want to give it but it is not mindfulness.

And when people say Buddhism is the new opium of the people or helps the corporate world we live in, they are not speaking of Buddhism as the Buddha taught it. They can call it whatever they like but it is not Buddhism. I write this as someone who is not attached to mindfulness even though I practice and teach it. I tell my classes almost every time I speak that if someone would invent a pill that allowed me to effectively manage the bewildering creations of my mind, with no side effects, leaving me free to think clearly and compassionately, I'd take it straight away and dump all the challenging thing I have to do to be as mindful as possible. And I am not Buddhist, so have no attachment to it either.

Deeply Programmed by the Past

I was curious about what happened in history on this day 26th August. I looked up the date on Wikipedia and they had an enormous list of things that had happened. The list added to a question I had been thinking about for the last few years, and especially recently while I've been watching a fascinating history of Ireland on BBC 4. That is, are we all carrying the suffering and trauma of countless generations in our genes, our DNA, our minds?

The scientific evidence about DNA and genes is mixed and disputed. But what we do know is that the behaviour of our parents or whoever raised you does have an effect on us, and they in turn had been affected by the attitude and actions of their parents or carers, and so on back in time for as long as our species has existed.

So even if the effect of events aren't passed on in our genes, we are almost certainly affected by our parents' own life experiences. Looking at the Wikipedia list of events in history I counted 35 in total, of which 20 are about killings, battles or wars. Watching the history of Ireland – I'm up to the reign of Queen Elizabeth I – much of it concerns invasions, massacres, and starvation. Survivors of these events who went on to have children obviously carried some aspects of what they witnessed or experienced in how they behaved day to day.

Given the sheer scale and frequency of such awful acts, it is reasonable to assume that our ancestors passed on at the very least behaviours affected by these events. This in addition to the normal suffering of human life though the ages; infant and child mortality, death of mothers in childbirth, death from famine, death from disease.

Not exactly cheery stuff for a mindfulness column you may think, but this is about who we really are, which is to say, our own thoughts from moment to moment, what those thoughts are, whether they are rational or not, whether they are helpful or unhelpful in our lives, whether they are considerate and compassionate or cold and brutal.

These thoughts, reactions, prejudices and mental habits don't appear from nowhere. They are the results of your genes and your past. That's the only places they can come from.

So what can we do about this, if we are all essentially programmed by past events and past people?

Firstly we can understand that this is the case. That helps us stop blaming ourselves for our imperfection. That's a good thing in itself because berating yourself helps no one.

Secondly we can stop blaming others for how we feel. Why? Because, like you, they act as they do because they are also the results of their past events and past people, and have limited if any control over who they have become.

That's hard for some people to accept but the science is very strong in this area. Moreover, like blaming yourself, blaming others does you no good, and does you a heap of harm because it makes you bitter, which you carry around with you, weighing you down, and making you negative for the rest of your days.

Now we can start to do something about all this accumulated stuff that our past events and our ancestors have heaped on us. Mindfulness is not a quick fix nor is it a pill that cures all ills, but it does work, especially if you work at it.

It's not just about the practice called mindful meditation where we either try to focus on one thing single-pointedly, usually the breath, or else just observe whatever contents our mind has at that time. This helps but equally if not more important is to try to become more and more aware of as many moments in your life as possible. Deliberately aware, not just automatically thinking or feeling this or that, and being dragged to wherever your volatile, unpredictable mind happens to drag you.

When you take a sip of water notice fully the experience of sipping the water. When you laugh at something funny on Facebook or TV be totally absorbed in the humour. If you feel fresh air on your face, really experience it. Don't think about it, don't analyse it, just completely be it as if that is all you are at that moment, just a living thing feeling the wind hit the skin on your face.

The result of doing your moments like this instead of worrying, planning, ruminating or regretting, which is what we usually do, is that the mind mellows, and it starts to really enjoy and appreciate these everyday experiences.

In the long run this helps to mitigate, even eliminate some of the destructive junk we have built up since we were born. All the ancestral centuries of pain, fear, hatred, worry, anxiety lying dormant in your mind, ready to flare up in reaction to the tiniest of events, can be kept quieter, or gently dealt with by a single change of attention to the clear feeling of an inbreath, then the peaceful calmness of the out-breath.

This is how we tame the inner demons from our own lives, and the lives of all those who came before us. And if we can collectively learn to do this as a species we can perhaps in time stop adding to that long list of wars, battles and barbarous events which have so harmed the lives of those who came before us and many who still suffer today.

What's your Philosophy?

You do have a philosophy of life and you live by it pretty rigorously. You might not know you have and that's because your philosophy has slowly but surely developed over all the years you have been alive.

What is a philosophy of life? It's your understanding of what your life is for, and how to live it. For the last two thousand years and more most people's philosophies of life were literally dictated to them by religious leaders and teachers. Rabbis, Hindu gurus, Buddhist monks, Taoist teachers, Popes and bishops and priests, imams, druid priests, elders of myriad tribes across all the continents. They taught either oral traditional teaching about what life was, and how to adhere to the right way of living, or did so from sacred texts, ascribed ultimately to God or Gods or some great being, usually though not always non-human.

These teachings became the philosophy for billions of people in the past, and are still the fundamental guides to living for billions in our own age. However it is instructive to look at how precisely an individual comes to accept or absorb such a way of seeing life. After all, we aren't born following a religion or philosophy.

Or are we? Well, not quite. There is some evidence suggesting that certain genes may lead some people to be more likely to adopt a religious way of seeing life than others, though this is not universally agreed amongst scientists in that field.

Far more clear is the relationship between parents' or other carers' beliefs and the likelihood of their children being brought up under the same belief system. In other words, with no negative connotation intended, children are conditioned to believe the same as their parents in very many cases.

Even children who are brought up by people who studiously try not to condition their children about religion, atheism or agnosticism still do condition their children about what life is for and how we should live it. That's because children pick up on their carers' every word, every gesture, every facial expression, and every act. In the early years they literally copy these because, other than their instincts lodged deep in the genes, it's the only way a young human can learn how to live.

At the risk of sounding overly paradoxical even having no philosophy of life is itself a philosophy. So whether we want one or not, and whether we were explicitly brought up to believe in one or not, we all have a philosophy, a way of thinking what life is for and how to live it well.

For most of us, second only to our parents or other carers' teachings and lifestyles, the culture within which we live has the most influence on how we see life. That could be the local culture, right down to street level, and all the way past national culture and values to the way the world seems to operate in our particular age.

We can't help but be influenced and programmed by these things. It's part of how the brain develops, something called neuroplasticity. This means that every experience you have enters the brain and is added to the sum total of experiences, including the genes you got at conception. The more the same things are experienced, the stronger a perception they create in your mind. This is how we learn skills like driving, riding a bike, even how to hold your knife and fork at dinner.

Not everything we experience can be positive. Life's not like that for anyone. So unhelpful, unhealthy or undeniably harmful views and events enter the sum total contents of your brain, and become a part of you. How much and how unhelpful depends on your unique brain. Everyone is different. Some of us are born lucky with more helpful genes than others. Some are born lucky with parents who are wise and loving. Some are luckier still because they get all this and their parents live in a safe, compassionate society and community. Tragically others have the opposite, a rough series of bad fortune, none of it their fault.

All of this is what makes us who we are, and how we see life and think of it – that's your philosophy.

Where mindfulness fits in on all this is to help us notice much more clearly how we actually see our life, what we think it's for, and how we live it moment by moment, day in, day out. That's stage one, getting to know our mind deeply. This obviously includes seeing our many unhelpful or destructive ways of thinking and doing.

An example is being sarcastic to those around us, something I used to do a lot when I was young. Sarcasm stems from two urges; the urge to be noticed by others, and the urge to cause a minor hurt to another. In other words a combination of egotism and malice.

Egotism reflects a philosophy of "me first" or "me only" whilst malice is part of a philosophy that states it is OK to cause harm to others if we benefit from it.

Mindfulness helps us see how our behaviour fits into positive and negative philosophical ways of seeing and doing life.

Stage two is developing the skill of letting go of destructive thoughts, urges, habits as they arise. We do this in one of two ways; by calmly waiting for the thought to weaken and fade away naturally, which usually takes less than ten seconds, or by changing our focus onto something more constructive or pleasant, often the breath.

It's hard to imagine but doing this regularly and calmly will in the long run change your philosophy to one that reflects clarity of thought, calmness of response to life, and compassionate towards others.

Printed in Poland
by Amazon Fulfillment
Poland Sp. z o.o., Wrocław

50835766R00186